How Being a Christian Made Me a Great HR Leader

How Being a Christian Made Me a Great HR Leader

Marisol Valle

Published by MARISOL VALLE, 2024.

HOW BEING A CHRISTIAN MADE ME A GREAT HR LEADER

First edition. December 7, 2024.

Copyright © 2024 Marisol Valle.

ISBN: 979-8230708407

Written by Marisol Valle.

Dedication

To my husband, Elvin Sr, and my children, Elvin Jr and Ashley, whose unwavering love and support have been the bedrock of my life and career. Your patience, understanding, and encouragement have sustained me through countless challenges, reminding me daily of the importance of family and faith. This book is a testament to the power of family, a reflection of our shared journey, and a heartfelt expression of my gratitude for your constant presence in my life.

Your faith, your love, and your belief in me have been a constant source of strength and inspiration, pushing me forward when I felt I could go no further. This journey would have been impossible without your steadfast love and unwavering support. This book is as much yours as it is mine.

Preface

This book is not just a collection of HR strategies and leadership tips; it's a deeply personal account of how my faith has shaped my career. For years, I navigated the complexities of HR, leading teams that grew from 500 to 2500 employees. I faced countless challenges—difficult employees, ethical dilemmas, organizational conflicts, and the ever-present pressure to perform. Through it all, my faith in God served as my compass, guiding my decisions, and sustaining me in moments of doubt and uncertainty.

THIS JOURNEY WASN'T always easy. Balancing faith, family, and a demanding career required constant prayer, careful planning, and a healthy dose of grace. I made mistakes along the way, learned invaluable lessons, and discovered the profound impact that integrating Christian values can have on leadership and team building. In sharing my story, I hope to inspire and equip fellow HR professionals, regardless of their faith background, to embrace ethical leadership, build stronger teams, and foster positive work environments.

I BELIEVE THAT THE principles of servant leadership, empathy, integrity, and forgiveness – principles deeply rooted in my faith – are not just Christian values, they are universal principles that drive success in any organization. My prayer is that this book will provide both practical strategies and inspirational insights for your leadership journey.

Introduction

The path to becoming a successful HR leader is often paved with challenges. Negotiating complex personnel issues, managing organizational change, and building high-performing teams requires resilience, empathy, and a clear ethical compass. For me, that compass has always been my faith. This book explores the intersection of my Christian faith and my HR career, revealing how integrating my beliefs into my professional life transformed my approach to leadership, coaching, hiring, and employee relations.

IT'S A STORY OF GROWTH, both professionally and spiritually, a testament to the transformative power of faith in the workplace. Throughout these pages, you'll find practical strategies and relatable anecdotes, weaving together my personal journey with actionable advice for HR professionals of all backgrounds. We'll delve into the art of asking the right interview questions, fostering effective communication, and building bridges between employees and management.

You'll learn how to navigate ethical dilemmas, cultivate a culture of care, and lead with

empathy, even during times of crisis. The book also addresses the unique challenges faced when scaling teams, maintaining a positive company culture during periods of rapid growth (as my experience from 500 to 2500 employees can attest), and empowering employees while upholding ethical standards. Ultimately, this book is a call to action, an invitation to reflect on your own leadership style and explore the potential for integrating your personal values, whatever they may be, into your professional life.

It's about discovering the power of purpose-driven leadership and creating workplaces where both employees and organizations thrive. My hope is that this book will inspire you to lead with integrity, compassion, and a deep sense of purpose.

Early Career Challenges and Spiritual Awakening

My early career in Human Resources was, to put it mildly, a baptism by fire. Landing a junior HR position at a rapidly growing startup, I quickly discovered that the realities of the workplace were worlds apart from the structured scenarios I had imagined.

Instead of clear processes and collaborative teams, I faced a whirlwind of interpersonal conflicts, undefined roles, and relentless performance expectations—all without adequate training or guidance.

The first few months were a blur of long hours, demanding managers, and an ever-present sense of being in over my head. I grappled with challenges I felt unprepared to tackle, often questioning whether I had what it took to succeed in such a high-pressure environment.

Burnout loomed like a constant shadow, particularly during one exhausting week where I was juggling a contentious disciplinary hearing, a sensitive redundancy process, and a mountain of administrative tasks. These experiences pushed me to the brink but ultimately shaped my resilience and adaptability, setting the stage for my growth as an HR professional. The pressure was immense, leaving me feeling emotionally drained and questioning my capabilities. My initial enthusiasm quickly waned, replaced by a growing sense of despair.

I began to doubt my abilities, my career choice, and even my future. The relentless pace and the constant challenges seemed insurmountable. This period of intense pressure and professional uncertainty became the catalyst for a profound shift in my life. While I'd always considered myself a Christian, my faith had largely remained a private, Sunday-morning affair, separate from the intense demands of my professional life. In the midst of the chaos, however, I found myself increasingly turning to prayer – not just for personal comfort, but also for guidance in navigating the complex situations I faced.

This wasn't a sudden, dramatic conversion; it was a gradual, organic process. Initially, my prayers were fueled by desperation, seeking divine intervention to help me overcome the immediate hurdles. I would spend evenings poring over scripture, seeking solace and wisdom in the stories of faith and resilience. Gradually, however, I began to notice a subtle shift in my perspective. Instead of viewing challenges as insurmountable obstacles, I started to see them as

opportunities for growth and learning.

The difficult conversations, the conflict resolution sessions, even the administrative nightmares – all became opportunities to apply my faith in practical ways. This newfound spiritual perspective began to transform my approach to HR. For instance, I found myself naturally gravitating towards empathy in my interactions with

employees. Instead of simply following procedures, I started paying attention to the emotional and spiritual needs of the individuals I worked with. A sensitive employee experiencing personal hardship, for example, was met not just with a standard HR response, but with genuine care and compassion.

I started seeing the people I interacted with not as mere cogs in a corporate machine, but as individuals with unique stories, struggles, and potential. This shift in perspective wasn't merely a personal choice; it was rooted in my understanding of Christian principles, particularly the teachings of Christ regarding love, compassion, and forgiveness. I began actively seeking ways to apply these principles to my work, viewing every interaction as an opportunity to reflect God's love and grace.

ONE PARTICULAR INCIDENT vividly illustrates this change. The company was facing a period of rapid expansion, leading to significant pressure on existing teams. Morale was low, and conflicts were erupting frequently. Instead of resorting to disciplinary measures, as many in my position may have done, I felt a strong urge to create a space for open communication and reconciliation. I organized team-building activities focused on collaboration and shared goals, incorporating elements of forgiveness and understanding, drawing upon the examples from the Bible.

The transformation was gradual, but significant. Over time, the atmosphere within the teams shifted from one of tension and resentment to one of collaboration and mutual respect. Open communication became the norm, and conflicts were resolved with greater empathy and understanding. The success of this initiative reaffirmed the power of faith-based principles in the workplace. While I didn't preach or proselytize, the impact of my actions – born out of my faith– was undeniable.

My commitment to fairness, my willingness to listen without judgment, and my genuine care for my colleagues fostered an environment of trust and mutual respect that contributed directly to improved productivity, reduced conflict, and enhanced team cohesion. This newfound approach also significantly impacted my ability to resolve conflicts. In my earlier days, confrontations felt intimidating, and my responses were often reactive, fueled by a desire to maintain order rather than to understand the root causes of the conflict.

With a deeper faith, however, I discovered the power of seeking reconciliation and restorative justice. I learned to approach each conflict with prayer, seeking guidance and wisdom in navigating complex situations. I employed active listening skills, striving to understand the perspective of each party involved. The emphasis shifted from assigning blame to seeking mutual understanding and solutions. I adopted a more patient, forgiving approach, recognizing that people make mistakes, and that genuine reconciliation often requires empathy, grace, and a willingness to forgive.

This newfound approach not only led to more effective conflict resolution, but also deepened my relationships with colleagues and enhanced the overall morale within the teams. The transition wasn't without its challenges. Balancing faith, family, and a demanding career proved to be a constant juggling act. There were many late nights, missed family dinners, and the ever-present feeling of not doing enough in any area. The guilt weighed heavily at times. However, through this struggle, I discovered the importance of effective time management, setting clear boundaries, and actively seeking support from family and friends.

Openly sharing my challenges and seeking guidance from trusted mentors, including my spouse and fellow Christians, proved invaluable. My family became my greatest source of encouragement and strength, providing the love, support, and understanding needed to navigate this challenging phase.

We developed strategies for managing my workload,
prioritizing tasks, and making time for family. This included setting specific times for work, family time, and spiritual practices, creating a balanced routine that helped prevent burnout.

Through prayer, scripture study, and seeking counsel from mentors and faith-based colleagues, I discovered effective strategies for managing stress and maintaining my well-being. These included incorporating mindfulness practices, engaging in physical exercise, and creating time for rest and relaxation. This wasn't a matter of simply adding more tasks to an already overflowing schedule; it was a conscious decision to prioritize self-care as a vital component of my overall wellness.

RECOGNIZING MY LIMITATIONS and seeking help when needed became an essential part of my leadership journey. My faith taught me the importance of humility, admitting my own weaknesses and seeking guidance from others. This wasn't a sign of weakness, but rather a strength, a willingness to acknowledge my limitations and seek the support necessary to overcome challenges. The integration of my faith into my professional life wasn't a passive process; it was an active, intentional choice.

I ACTIVELY SOUGHT OPPORTUNITIES to incorporate my values into every aspect of my work, from hiring practices to conflict resolution, from performance evaluations to strategic planning. This active integration provided me with a clear moral compass, a guiding principle that helped me navigate the complexities of the corporate world. My faith provided me with an inner resilience and strength to persevere through challenges and setbacks and gave me a sense of purpose that went beyond personal ambition.

THIS PROFOUND TRANSFORMATION didn't happen overnight; it was a gradual, evolving process, shaped by both my professional experiences and my deepening spiritual journey. But the impact was undeniable: it radically altered my approach to leadership, improved my effectiveness as an HR professional, and enriched both my personal and professional life. The early struggles, the periods of intense pressure and self-doubt, ultimately became steppingstones on my path to finding both professional fulfillment and spiritual growth.

THIS INTEGRATION BECAME the bedrock upon which I built a successful and rewarding career in HR, a journey I share in the following chapters.

Balancing Faith Family and Career

The transition from a struggling junior HR professional to a confident leader wasn't solely about mastering technical skills; it was profoundly influenced by my commitment to integrating my faith into every facet of my life.

This included, most importantly, finding a healthy balance between my faith, my family, and my demanding career. This wasn't a simple equation; it required constant recalibration, adjustments, and a willingness to prioritize differently depending on the season of life. Initially, the lines blurred considerably. The long hours and intense pressure of my early career often left me feeling depleted, with little energy left for my family. My husband, Elvin Sr., bore the brunt of this imbalance. He understood the pressures of my career but also saw the toll it was taking on our relationship and our young children.

He became my rock, providing unwavering support and encouragement, even when I felt like giving up. His faith in me, both professionally and spiritually, was instrumental in keeping me grounded during those turbulent times. We learned, often through trial and error, the importance of establishing clear boundaries. This meant setting specific work hours, resisting the urge to constantly check emails after hours, and consciously disconnecting on weekends to fully engage with family.

IT ALSO MEANT LEARNING to say "no" to additional responsibilities, when necessary, a lesson that took time and practice to master. Initially, I felt immense guilt at declining extra work, fearing that it would negatively impact my career progression. However, I realized that burnout wouldn't benefit anyone, least of all my employer. A refreshed and focused employee is far more valuable than one perpetually teetering on the brink of collapse. This realization was a turning point. By protecting my personal time, I enhanced my productivity and efficiency during working hours.

ESTABLISHING A DEDICATED family time ritual became crucial. Evenings often involved a family dinner, followed by a dedicated time for reading, playing games, or simply talking. Weekends were reserved for family outings, church activities, or simply relaxing at home. These moments became sacred, untouchable spaces where we focused entirely on each other, strengthening our bonds and providing a much-needed counterpoint to the pressures of my work. We also found that incorporating our faith into these family times was profoundly beneficial.

REGULAR FAMILY PRAYERS, Bible studies, and discussions about spiritual matters helped us navigate challenges together and maintain a shared sense of purpose. This wasn't about imposing religion but about sharing our values and beliefs, fostering open communication, and building a strong spiritual foundation for our family. My children, Elvin Jr and Ashley also played a significant role in this journey. Witnessing my dedication to both my career and my family taught them the importance of balance and commitment. They learned that success wasn't just about achieving professional goals but also about nurturing relationships and maintaining a strong moral compass.

IT WASN'T ALWAYS EASY; there were times when work demands conflicted with school events or family trips. However, we developed strategies for navigating these conflicts, prioritizing what was most important and communicating openly with each other. Sometimes, this meant making difficult choices – missing a work event to attend a child's school play or postponing a business trip to attend a family emergency. These choices, while sometimes challenging, reinforced our values and strengthened our family bonds. They showed my children that family always came first, even during times of high professional pressure.

FURTHERMORE, SEEKING mentorship and support from other Christian leaders was instrumental in maintaining this delicate balance. I found a community of fellow believers who understood the unique challenges of integrating faith and career, providing invaluable advice, encouragement, and accountability. They were a source of wisdom, sharing their experiences and offering practical strategies for managing time, setting boundaries, and prioritizing family.

THEIR SUPPORT HELPED me navigate difficult decisions and maintain perspective during challenging times. These relationships weren't just professional networking; they were true friendships built on shared faith and mutual respect. They served as a vital support system, understanding the emotional and spiritual toll that my demanding career could take. Time management became an essential skill. I implemented various strategies, including prioritizing tasks, delegating responsibilities, utilizing technology effectively, and

LEARNING TO SAY "NO" to non-essential commitments. I experimented with different time-management techniques, like the Pomodoro Technique, and discovered what worked best for my

personality and work style. The key was finding a system that helped me stay organized, focused, and efficient, allowing me to dedicate adequate time to both my work and my family without feeling constantly overwhelmed. This involved being incredibly disciplined, learning to delegate effectively, and using technology to my advantage.

I relied heavily on calendar apps to schedule appointments, set reminders, and ensure that I didn't overcommit myself. I also learned to use email efficiently, responding promptly to urgent requests while filtering out less important messages to avoid information overload. Beyond time management, prayer and meditation became essential components of my daily routine. These practices provided me with the spiritual strength, clarity, and peace necessary to navigate the complexities of my life. It was during these moments of quiet reflection that I gained

perspective, seeking guidance from God in making difficult decisions and maintaining a balanced approach to my work and family life. I also found solace in studying scripture, drawing inspiration and wisdom from the lives of biblical figures who faced their own trials and tribulations. These practices weren't just religious exercises; they were a source of strength, resilience, and inner peace that enabled me to withstand the pressures of my demanding career and maintain a healthy relationship with my family.

THE JOURNEY OF BALANCING faith, family, and career has been a continuous learning process. There have been setbacks and moments of doubt, times when I felt overwhelmed and inadequate. However, my faith has been my anchor, providing me with the strength and resilience to persevere. The support of my husband, my children, and my faith community has been invaluable, enabling me to find a fulfilling balance between my personal and professional life. The result hasn't been perfect, but it's been deeply rewarding.

I'VE LEARNED THAT TRUE success isn't just about climbing the corporate ladder, but about living a life of purpose, integrity, and meaningful relationships. This integrated approach to life has not only enriched my personal life but has also significantly impacted my effectiveness as an HR leader. The principles of empathy, compassion, and servant leadership, deeply rooted in my faith, have become the cornerstones of my leadership style, enabling me to build strong, supportive teams and foster a positive and productive work environment.

The journey continues, and the challenges will inevitably evolve, but the foundation of faith, family, and a balanced perspective remain my guiding principles. This integrated approach has not just improved my work-life balance but has truly enhanced my effectiveness as a leader, proving that a life rooted in faith can indeed lead to remarkable success in all aspects of life. It's a testament to the power of integrating faith into one's professional life, a journey that continues to unfold, shaping both my professional and personal growth.

The ongoing process of prioritizing, adapting, and seeking guidance is a testament to the dynamic nature of balancing these crucial elements of life. The rewards, however, far outweigh the challenges, resulting in a fulfilling and purposeful life, both professionally and personally.

A Christian Principle

My understanding of leadership underwent a radical transformation as I delved deeper into my faith. The traditional, hierarchical model of leadership, where authority flowed top-down, felt increasingly at odds with the teachings of Christ.

The Gospels portray a radically different leader—one who washes the feet of his disciples, who serves rather than commands, who prioritizes the needs of the least among us. This image profoundly resonated with my own desire to lead with empathy and compassion.

It became clear that servant leadership, rooted in the life and teachings of Jesus, was not just a desirable ideal but a fundamental principle for effective and ethical leadership in any context, especially in the demanding world of human resources.

Servant leadership, as I came to understand it, isn't about weakness or subservience. It's about prioritizing the growth and well-being of your team members above your own ambitions. It's about empowering others, listening attentively to their concerns, and creating an environment where everyone feels valued and respected. It's about leading with humility, acknowledging your own limitations, and seeking input and collaboration from those you lead. It's about recognizing that true leadership is about serving others, not wielding power over them.

This concept, deeply rooted in Christian principles of love, humility, and selflessness, became the cornerstone of my approach to managing teams. This shift in perspective was initially challenging. My earlier management style, though not overtly authoritarian, had been shaped by the conventional corporate ethos. I had focused on achieving results, often prioritizing efficiency over empathy. I measured success largely by metrics and targets. However, the servant leadership model challenged this.

I FOUND MYSELF NEEDING to consciously retrain my approach, replacing a focus on purely quantitative results with a more holistic perspective which included the well-being and development of my team. This transition involved actively listening to my team members, seeking to understand their individual needs and aspirations. It meant creating opportunities for professional development and growth, empowering them to take ownership of their work and make decisions autonomously.

IT MEANT FOSTERING open communication, creating a safe space where individuals felt comfortable sharing their concerns and feedback without fear of reprisal. This shift required a significant investment in building relationships, spending time getting to know each team member beyond their job title and performance metrics. I began to appreciate the unique strengths and talents of each person, realizing that a diverse team was not simply an asset but a vital ingredient for success.

ONE PARTICULAR INSTANCE stands out. Our company was undergoing a significant restructuring, a process which naturally caused considerable anxiety among the employees. Instead of simply disseminating information top-down, which would have led to confusion and uncertainty, I opted for a transparent and participatory approach. I held numerous small group meetings where individuals could freely express their concerns, ask questions, and provide feedback. I listened attentively, acknowledging the validity of their fears and anxieties.

By creating a safe space for dialogue, I was able to address many misunderstandings and mitigate much of the apprehension. The subsequent restructuring process was surprisingly smooth, largely thanks to the trust and collaboration we had built through open communication and mutual understanding. This entire process mirrored the Christian principle of caring for the flock, of shepherding those in your charge with empathy and compassion. Moreover, servant leadership extends beyond just internal team dynamics.

It encompasses building positive relationships with external stakeholders, clients, and partners. Treating everyone with respect, integrity, and fairness, regardless of their position or status, is not merely good business practice; it is a reflection of Christian values of love and compassion. In my experience, fostering strong relationships with external stakeholders has led to improved collaboration, trust, and mutual respect. Another significant aspect of servant leadership is the ability to delegate effectively.

This isn't simply about assigning tasks; it's about empowering individuals to take on responsibility, to develop their skills, and to exercise their judgment. I learned the importance of providing support and guidance without micromanaging. Trusting my team members to handle their responsibilities not only frees up my time to focus on strategic initiatives but also fosters a sense of ownership and accountability among them. This aligns directly with the principle of empowering others, providing opportunities for growth and development, and encouraging their individual talents to flourish. Of course, implementing servant leadership hasn't been without its challenges.

IT REQUIRES A SIGNIFICANT shift in mindset, a willingness to let go of control, and a commitment to prioritize the needs of others.

There have been times when I've questioned my own effectiveness, wondering if my focus on team well-being was compromising the achievement of organizational goals. However, I've consistently found that a team empowered and supported thrives and outperforms a team that is solely focused on delivering targets. The increased morale, loyalty, and productivity far outweigh any perceived losses in short-term efficiency.

FURTHERMORE, SERVANT leadership isn't a static concept; it's a continuous journey of learning and growth. I constantly seek opportunities to refine my approach, to learn from my mistakes, and to adapt my style to meet the evolving needs of my team and the organization.

Regular self-reflection, seeking feedback from my team members and peers, and actively seeking guidance from my faith community all play a vital role in this ongoing process. The integration of servant leadership into my management style has not only strengthened my teams but has also enriched my own life. It

has allowed me to experience the immense satisfaction of empowering others, of witnessing their growth and development, and of contributing to a more positive and fulfilling work environment. It has strengthened my faith, reminding me that true leadership is about service, not power. This deep connection between my faith and my professional life has proven to be a source of strength, resilience, and profound meaning. The journey to becoming a truly effective servant leader is ongoing. It requires ongoing learning, constant self-reflection, and a commitment to living out Christian principles in the workplace. However, the rewards—a more engaged, productive, and fulfilled team, and a deeper sense of purpose and meaning in my own life—are immeasurable. It's a testament to the transformative power of faith, proving that a life lived with integrity and compassion can lead to exceptional professional success and genuine personal fulfillment. The lessons learned resonate not only in my professional life but in my personal life as well, enriching both my relationships with my family and my broader community.

The journey is a testament to the powerful synergy between faith and leadership, a blend that has shaped me into a more effective leader and a more fulfilled individual. This has been, and continues to be, the most rewarding path I've ever chosen. The consistent application of these principles, guided by faith and a commitment to servant leadership, has not only built strong teams but also fostered a culture of trust, respect, and mutual support, a cornerstone of any successful organization.

OVERCOMING OBSTACLES with Faith as a Guide

The transition from a company of 500 employees to one boasting over 2500 wasn't a smooth, linear ascent. It was more like scaling a treacherous mountain range, each peak representing a new and unforeseen challenge. My faith, however, became my unwavering compass, guiding me through the storms and ensuring I didn't lose sight of my ethical compass, even amidst the chaos. One such storm involved a particularly difficult employee, Sarah.

SARAH WAS INCREDIBLY talented, a true asset to the marketing team, but her interpersonal skills left much to be desired. She clashed repeatedly with colleagues, creating a toxic environment within her department. Traditional HR approaches—written warnings, performance improvement plans—had proven ineffective. Her behavior persisted, threatening to undermine team morale and productivity. Initially, my frustration mounted. I felt the pressure of maintaining productivity and a positive work environment.

THE TEMPTATION TO RESORT to disciplinary action, perhaps even termination, was strong. However, I paused, remembering the teachings of Christ on forgiveness and compassion. I prayed for guidance, seeking wisdom beyond my own limited understanding. The answer came not as a resounding voice but as a quiet prompting within my heart: seek to understand, not just to judge. Instead of focusing on Sarah's flaws, I scheduled a private meeting with her, not to reprimand, but to listen.

I APPROACHED THE CONVERSATION with empathy, creating a safe space for her to express her frustrations and concerns. To my surprise, Sarah's abrasive behavior stemmed from deep-seated insecurities and a fear of failure. She felt overwhelmed by her responsibilities and lacked confidence in her abilities. This revelation shifted my perspective entirely. My role wasn't simply to enforce company policies but to help Sarah to nurture her talent while addressing her shortcomings. This meant taking a different approach.

I worked with Sarah to develop a tailored mentorship program, pairing her with a supportive senior colleague who could guide her, both professionally and emotionally. We also provided her with additional training to improve her communication skills and conflict-resolution techniques. The transformation was gradual but remarkable. Sarah's interactions with colleagues improved significantly. Her productivity soared as her confidence grew. Her story became a powerful example within the company, highlighting the transformative potential of understanding, compassion, and faith-based leadership.

It reinforced the importance of seeing people as individuals, recognizing their inherent worth, and extending grace even in challenging situations. This experience deeply impacted my leadership style, reminding me to always prioritize empathy and understanding in my interactions with employees. Another significant obstacle involved a major conflict between two departments—engineering and sales. The conflict had been simmering for months, escalating into a bitter rivalry that threatened to paralyze the company. The tension was palpable, permeating every meeting and interaction between the two teams. The root of the conflict lay in differing priorities and communication breakdowns. Engineering felt undervalued and underappreciated, believing sales consistently placed unrealistic demands on their capabilities. Sales, conversely, felt that engineering was slow to respond to their needs, jeopardizing their ability to meet sales targets. Both sides were entrenched in their positions, refusing to compromise. Traditional conflict-resolution methods seemed inadequate.

Mediation attempts had failed, leaving the situation increasingly volatile.

Once again, I turned to prayer, seeking divine guidance. This time, the answer felt less like a subtle prompting and more like a clear directive: facilitate open and honest communication, emphasizing the shared goal of the company's success. I organized a series of facilitated workshops bringing together members from both departments. The goal wasn't simply to resolve the immediate conflict but to foster a culture of mutual respect and understanding. We used activities and exercises designed to encourage empathy and perspective-taking.

Team members shared their personal experiences, highlighting the challenges they faced and the impact of their actions on others. The atmosphere was surprisingly receptive. As individuals began to understand each other's perspectives, the resentment began to dissipate. The workshops weren't a quick fix; they required commitment and patience. But gradually, a sense of shared purpose emerged. The teams started to collaborate more effectively, communicating openly and transparently. The initial hostility gave way to mutual respect and cooperation, ultimately strengthening the overall organizational performance and demonstrating that conflict can be a catalyst for growth if approached with faith and empathy. Throughout my journey, I've found that faith isn't a shield against challenges, but rather a source of strength and resilience in overcoming them. It equips me with the patience to persevere, the empathy to understand, and the wisdom to find creative solutions. It's not about ignoring problems or avoiding conflict; it's about facing them head-on, guided by a set of values that transcends the bottom line.

WHILE NAVIGATING THE complexities of organizational restructuring, budget constraints, and rapid growth, I've realized that faith isn't just a personal conviction; it's a powerful leadership principle.

It informs every decision I make, shaping my approach to team building, conflict resolution, and employee relations. One particular instance highlighted the practical application of faith-based leadership during a period of significant company restructuring. The decision to streamline operations led to inevitable job losses. This was one of the most difficult challenges I faced, ethically and emotionally. The traditional approach might have involved a swift, impersonal announcement, minimizing human interaction to prevent emotional outbursts. However, my faith compelled me to approach this situation with compassion. I believed that each employee deserved respect, dignity, and transparency, even in the face of unfortunate news. We organized individual meetings with each affected employee, allowing them to express their concerns and ask questions. We provided outplacement services, including resume writing workshops, job search support, and networking opportunities.

We also offered extended benefits and severance packages exceeding the standard company policy. This wasn't simply about complying with legal obligations; it was about demonstrating our commitment to the well-being of our employees, even as we made tough business decisions. The response was unexpected. While the sadness and disappointment were palpable, the employees expressed gratitude for the respectful and empathetic manner in which the situation was handled. Several individuals even shared their appreciation for the organization's commitment to treating them with dignity and care, despite the difficult circumstances.

This experience reinforced the belief that faith-based leadership, grounded in compassion and empathy, not only minimizes the negative impact of organizational change but can also strengthen the relationship between employer and employee, fostering trust and respect during even the most challenging of times. The journey of integrating faith into my professional life has been a continuous process of learning, self-reflection, and refinement.

It's not about imposing religious beliefs on others; it's about living out the principles of Christ—love, compassion, forgiveness, and service—in my daily interactions. These principles have become the cornerstone of my leadership style, influencing everything from hiring practices to conflict resolution. They have shaped my approach to team building, employee relations, and organizational change, creating a work environment characterized by trust, respect, and mutual support.

AND IT IS THROUGH THESE tangible results that I've witnessed the powerful synergy between faith and leadership, proving that a life lived with integrity and compassion can indeed lead to exceptional professional success and genuine personal fulfillment. The consistent application of these principles has not only built strong teams but also fostered a culture of trust, respect, and mutual support, a cornerstone of any successful organization.

THE JOURNEY HAS BEEN transformational, not only for my career but also for my personal life, enriching my relationships with my family and my broader community. This journey continues, and I'm continually learning how to refine my approach as a faith-driven HR leader. Each challenge becomes a lesson, each conflict an opportunity for growth and a testament to the power of faith in the workplace. The rewards are immeasurable; a more engaged, productive, and fulfilled team, a deeper sense of purpose and meaning in my own life, and a lasting impact on the lives of those I serve.

Building a Foundation of Integrity in HR

Building a foundation of integrity in HR, especially within a rapidly expanding organization, requires a deliberate and consistent approach. My faith provided the unwavering compass guiding my ethical decision-making, ensuring that even amidst the pressures of growth and the complexities of personnel management, I never compromised on my values. The transition from a team of 500 to over 2500 employees brought with it an exponential increase in the number of ethical dilemmas I faced.

These weren't simply minor infractions; they were situations that tested the very fabric of our organizational culture and challenged my commitment to fairness and justice. One such challenge involved a significant restructuring of our sales department. We were implementing a new CRM system, and the transition proved far more disruptive than anticipated. Several long-term sales representatives, accustomed to their old methods, openly resisted the change, expressing their frustrations through complaints, decreased productivity, and even acts of subtle sabotage.

THEIR RESISTANCE THREATENED not only the successful implementation of the new system but also the morale of the entire department. My initial instinct was to take a firm, disciplinary approach. I could have issued warnings, implemented performance improvement plans, or even initiated termination proceedings. These were the standard HR protocols, the methods I'd learned in my years of experience. However, something felt different this time. The situation demanded more than just a procedural response. It required a deeper understanding,

EMPATHY, AND A COMMITMENT to restorative justice.

I began by holding individual meetings with each of the resistant employees. I listened intently to their concerns, validating their anxieties and acknowledging the challenges the transition presented. I didn't dismiss their complaints as mere resistance to change; instead, I treated their concerns with respect and sought to understand the root causes of their dissatisfaction. In several cases, I discovered that their resistance stemmed not from malice but from fear—fear of losing their jobs, fear of not being able to adapt to the new

technology, and fear of being left behind. This process of listening and understanding allowed me to tailor my approach to each individual. For some, it involved providing additional training and support to help them master the new CRM system. For others, it meant providing reassurance and clarifying their roles within the new structure. In one instance, I discovered an employee struggling with a personal crisis that was significantly impacting their work. Addressing that underlying issue allowed me to help them regain their focus and productivity.

This holistic approach, informed by my faith's emphasis on compassion and understanding, proved far more effective than any

disciplinary action could have been. Another challenging situation involved allegations of workplace bullying. An employee, David, accused a senior manager, Susan, of consistently belittling him and undermining his work. The evidence was circumstantial whispers in the breakroom, subtle snide remarks overheard by colleagues.

There was no concrete proof, no written documentation, just the testimony of the accuser and the denial of the accused. This was a delicate situation that demanded careful investigation. My Christian faith taught me the importance of seeking truth and justice, ensuring fairness for both parties. Ignoring the allegations would have been a betrayal of David's trust, but acting hastily without sufficient evidence could have unfairly damaged Susan's career. I initiated a thorough investigation, speaking to multiple witnesses, reviewing emails and internal

COMMUNICATIONS, AND interviewing both David and Susan separately.

My approach wasn't accusatory; it was focused on gathering information, understanding perspectives, and establishing the facts. I listened to both sides, allowing them to express their feelings and perspectives without interruption. I treated them both with respect, reminding myself that regardless of the outcome, both David and Susan were individuals deserving of dignity and compassion. The investigation revealed a pattern of behavior on Susan's part that, while not explicitly illegal, constituted a

form of subtle bullying. It was a case of poor leadership, not intentional malice. This allowed me to address the situation constructively, focusing on restorative rather than punitive measures. Susan was offered coaching and leadership training to help her improve her interpersonal skills and develop a more inclusive leadership style. David received support and counseling to help him cope with the impact of the bullying. In both the restructuring and bullying scenarios, my approach was guided by several key principles rooted in my faith:

EMPATHY AND COMPASSION:

Understanding the perspectives and feelings of those involved is crucial for resolving conflict constructively. This approach builds trust and encourages open communication.

Truth and Justice:

Seeking the truth, regardless of its

implications, is paramount. This means conducting thorough investigations, hearing all sides, and ensuring fair treatment for all parties involved.

Forgiveness and Restoration:

Focus on restoration rather than retribution.

THIS AIMS TO HEAL RELATIONSHIPS, improve communication, and prevent future conflicts.

Servant Leadership:

Leading by serving the needs of others, putting their well-being and development before personal gain. These principles, interwoven with my HR expertise, have created a work environment where employees feel valued, respected, and supported. The integration of my faith into my professional life hasn't been about imposing religious beliefs; it's been about living out the values of Christ in my daily work.

This has resulted in a stronger, more cohesive, and productive workforce, a testament to the powerful synergy between faith and effective leadership. The consistent application of these principles extends beyond conflict resolution. They inform us about our hiring practices, our performance management systems, and our approach to organizational change. In hiring, we prioritize candidates who demonstrate integrity, empathy, and a commitment to teamwork.

OUR PERFORMANCE MANAGEMENT system focuses on continuous improvement and growth, encouraging employees to develop their talents and reach their full potential. Organizational change is handled with transparency and open communication, ensuring employees are informed and involved in the process. The growth from 500 to 2500 employees wasn't solely about numbers; it was about building a culture where every individual felt valued, respected, and empowered.

THIS WASN'T ACHIEVED overnight; it was the result of consistent effort, unwavering faith, and a commitment to ethical leadership. The challenges were numerous, the ethical dilemmas complex, but the principles guiding my actions remained constant: empathy, justice, forgiveness, and service. These principles, deeply rooted in my Christian faith, are not just abstract ideals but practical tools that have shaped my leadership style and contributed to building a thriving and successful organization.

THE JOURNEY CONTINUES, with new challenges and opportunities arising constantly. However, the foundational principles of integrity, compassion, and a commitment to servant leadership remain my unwavering compass, guiding me forward and ensuring that our workplace reflects the values I hold dear. The expansion also brought challenges in maintaining a cohesive organizational culture.

As the company grew, the risk of departmental silos and communication breakdowns increased. To counteract this, I implemented initiatives to foster collaboration and teamwork across departments. This included cross-functional projects, team-building activities, and regular communication channels that promoted information sharing and feedback. The emphasis was always on building relationships and breaking down barriers.

WE ALSO SAW AN INCREASE in diversity within the workforce, which brought its own set of challenges and opportunities. To create an inclusive environment, we implemented diversity and inclusion training programs, reviewed our hiring practices to ensure fairness and equity, and established employee resource groups to support diverse employee populations. This was crucial not just for legal compliance, but also for building a truly representative and inclusive workplace reflective of the broader community we serve. It was an opportunity to demonstrate in tangible ways the biblical principles of loving our neighbors and treating all with equal dignity and respect. Beyond the workplace itself, integrating faith into HR leadership extends to how I manage my work-life balance. This has been a journey of learning and continuous adaptation, recognizing that setting healthy boundaries and

PRIORITIZING FAMILY is essential to maintain a sustainable and fulfilling career. It's about finding that balance where my professional life nourishes my spiritual life and vice versa, ensuring that neither is neglected at the expense of the other. This aspect of my journey is perhaps the most personal, requiring continual self-reflection and a willingness to adjust my approach based on the evolving needs of my family and my spiritual growth.

It's a process of seeking wisdom and guidance, both from spiritual mentors and from experienced colleagues, and it's a testament to the enduring strength and resilience that faith provides when navigating the complex demands of a high-pressure, fast-paced career. The journey continues, and each day presents new opportunities for learning, growth, and living out my faith in the workplace.

Developing Faith Based Interview Questions

Developing effective interview questions is crucial for any hiring process, but when you're seeking to build a team that reflects your faith-based values, the approach needs a nuanced touch. The goal isn't to screen out candidates based on their religious beliefs – that would be both ethically wrong and legally problematic – but rather to identify individuals whose character and work ethic align with your organizational principles.

THIS REQUIRES CAREFUL consideration of the questions you ask and the underlying qualities you seek to uncover. Remember, the legal landscape surrounding hiring is complex. Questions that directly inquire about religious affiliation or practices are strictly prohibited. Instead, we need to focus on questions that indirectly assess values like integrity, compassion, teamwork, and a strong work ethic—qualities often deeply rooted in a faith-based worldview.

These questions should be phrased in a way that is both relevant to the job and respectful of all candidates, regardless of their background. Let's explore some examples. Instead of asking, "Are you a practicing Christian?", we might ask, "Describe a time you faced a significant ethical dilemma. How did you approach the situation, and what was the outcome?" This question probes the candidate's moral compass and decision-making process without directly referencing religion.

THE ANSWER WILL REVEAL whether they prioritize integrity and honesty, crucial values in any workplace, but especially one guided by faith. Similarly, instead of asking about church attendance, we could ask, "Tell me about a time you had to work collaboratively with a team to achieve a common goal. What was your role, and what challenges did you overcome?" This question assesses teamwork skills and problem-solving abilities, both crucial for a productive and harmonious work environment.

A candidate who readily displays collaboration, empathy, and perseverance, demonstrates attributes often associated with Christian values such as love, forgiveness, and perseverance. Another effective approach involves using situational

questions. For example, you might ask, "Imagine a scenario where a colleague makes a mistake that impacts the team's project. How would you respond, and what steps would you take to address the situation?" This reveals their approach to conflict resolution, accountability, and forgiveness—all values integral to a faith-based workplace. Do they approach the situation with compassion and a desire for reconciliation, or do they resort to judgment and blame?

Their response can provide valuable insight into their character.

The focus should always be on behavior-based questions.

Instead of asking about abstract beliefs, ask about past

experiences. For instance, you might ask, "Describe a time you demonstrated initiative and went above and beyond your responsibilities.

What motivated you?" This reveals their level of commitment, dedication, and sense of responsibility—qualities highly valued in many faith traditions. The "why" behind their actions is often as telling as the "what."

It is vital to remember that consistency is key.

All candidates should be asked the same questions, ensuring fairness and avoiding any perception of bias. The goal is not to find only "believers," but individuals whose character and values align with the organization's culture, regardless of their specific faith background. The interview process should be a conversation, not an interrogation, allowing candidates to showcase their strengths and demonstrate how their skills and values are a good fit for the role and the team. Furthermore, consider incorporating questions that assess resilience and perseverance.

Faith often requires patience and endurance, and these qualities translate well into the workplace. For example, "Describe a time you faced a significant challenge or setback.

How did you overcome it, and what did you learn from the experience?"

This question explores not just their problem-solving skills, but

also, their mental fortitude and capacity for growth—attributes valued in many faith-based cultures. Developing faith-based interview questions requires a

delicate balance. The questions should be designed to assess character and work ethic without violating legal regulations or

inadvertently discriminating against candidates based on their religious affiliation. It's crucial to remain mindful of the legal ramifications of asking inappropriate questions.

Consult with legal counsel to ensure your interview process complies with all applicable laws and regulations.

However, simply avoiding problematic questions isn't enough. We must proactively craft questions that reveal the qualities we seek.

Consider the following additional examples:

"Describe a time you had to make a difficult decision with limited information. How did you proceed, and what was the outcome?"

This assesses problem-solving skills under pressure, a crucial skill in many workplaces.

"Tell me about a time you failed. What did you learn from that experience?"

This reveals self-awareness, humility, and a capacity for growth, all valuable traits.

"Describe a situation where you had to work with someone with a very different personality or work style. How did you navigate that dynamic?"

This tests adaptability, patience, and conflict-resolution skills.

"Describe a time you had to go the extra mile to help a colleague or customer. What motivated you?"

This identifies a candidate's commitment, empathy, and willingness to serve. Remember to listen actively to the candidates' responses, not just for the words they use, but for the underlying values and motivations they reveal.

The goal is not just to find someone who can perform the job, but someone who embodies the values and culture of the organization. By carefully crafting your interview questions and focusing on the underlying qualities that reflect your faith-based values, you can build a strong, ethical, and high-performing team. Beyond the specific questions, the overall interview process should reflect your values.

Create a welcoming and respectful environment where candidates feel comfortable being themselves.

LISTEN ATTENTIVELY to their responses and demonstrate genuine interest in getting to know them as individuals. The interview should be a two-way street, allowing the candidate to learn about your organization and its values just as you assess their fit. By approaching the interview process with integrity, compassion, and a genuine desire to find the right person for the role, you can ensure that your hiring decisions reflect your faith-based values in a positive and legally compliant way.

THIS APPROACH FOSTERS a work environment that is not only productive but also ethically sound and spiritually enriching for all involved. The combination of thoughtfully designed questions, respectful interviewing practices, and a sincere commitment to ethical hiring ensures a process that honors both your values and the legal and ethical considerations of the workplace. It's about finding the right fit, not just the right qualifications.

IDENTIFYING CHARACTER Traits Aligned with Christian Values

Building a team that reflects Christian values isn't about imposing a religious test; it's about identifying individuals whose character aligns with principles of integrity, compassion, and teamwork. These qualities, while deeply rooted in faith, are also highly desirable in any workplace. They translate into increased productivity, improved morale, and a more positive work environment.

THE CHALLENGE LIES in effectively assessing these character traits during the hiring process, a process that must remain legally compliant and ethically sound. One key element is understanding the nuances of these values. Integrity, for example, goes beyond simply telling the truth. It encompasses honesty, accountability, and a strong moral compass. During interviews, look for evidence of consistent behavior aligned with these principles. Have they faced ethical dilemmas in the past? How did they respond?

DID THEY TAKE RESPONSIBILITY for their actions, even when mistakes were made? Open-ended questions encouraging detailed responses will be far more revealing than simple yes or no questions.

For example, instead of asking, "Are you honest?", try asking, "Describe a time you had to make

a difficult decision with ethical implications. What was the situation, and how did you approach it?" Their response will offer a deeper insight into their character than a simple affirmation of honesty.

COMPASSION, ANOTHER crucial element, involves empathy, kindness, and a genuine concern for others. This is reflected in how they interact with colleagues, clients, and even competitors. Interview questions focused on teamwork and collaboration can illuminate a candidate's capacity for compassion. Ask about their experiences working on teams, specifically focusing on challenging situations where conflict arose. How did they contribute to resolving the conflict?

DID THEY DEMONSTRATE understanding and empathy towards others' perspectives? Did they prioritize the team's success over personal gain?

Their responses will reveal their ability to work collaboratively and support their team members. Look for evidence of active listening and a willingness to consider alternative viewpoints. A truly compassionate individual will be able to put themselves in others' shoes and understand their perspectives, even if they don't agree with them. Teamwork is essential in any successful organization, but it's particularly important when building a team grounded in Christian values. Christian teachings emphasize community and mutual support, which translates directly into effective teamwork in the workplace. Assessing a candidate's teamwork skills goes beyond simply asking if they're a team player. Instead, probe deeper into their experiences. Ask for specific examples of successful teamwork, highlighting their contributions and the challenges they overcame. Explore how they handle conflict within a team setting, focusing on their communication style, conflict-resolution skills, and ability to compromise. Did they actively participate in brainstorming sessions?

Did they take the initiative to assist team members? Did they accept constructive criticism and learn from their mistakes?

These aspects of teamwork showcase a commitment to collaboration and mutual support, which are essential for a thriving work environment. Beyond specific questions, the interview process itself should reflect your values. Create a welcoming and respectful environment where candidates feel comfortable being themselves. Show genuine interest in learning about their experiences and perspectives, demonstrating active listening and empathy throughout the conversation.

AVOID INTERRUPTING or dominating the conversation; instead, focus on fostering a dialogue that allows them to showcase their strengths and experiences fully. Remember that the interview is a two-way street; it's an opportunity for candidates to learn about your organization and its culture as well as for you to assess their fit. By demonstrating these values in your interviewing style, you are creating a more authentic and engaging experience for both the candidate and yourself.

This process requires keen observation of nonverbal cues as well. Body language, tone of voice, and eye contact can often reveal more than words alone. Observe how the candidate interacts with you and your team.

Do they maintain appropriate eye contact? Do they seem genuinely interested in the conversation? Is their body language open and welcoming or closed off and defensive? Pay attention to these subtle cues, as they can often reveal underlying character traits that might not be readily apparent in their verbal responses.

Combine your observations with the responses to your thoughtful questions and you will get a much more comprehensive view of the candidate's true nature and their alignment with your organizational values. Furthermore, it's important to consider the context of their previous work experience. While past performance doesn't guarantee future success, it does offer valuable insights into a candidate's character. Have they consistently demonstrated integrity in their past roles?

HAVE THEY BEEN A SUPPORTIVE and collaborative team member? Have they shown empathy and concern for their colleagues and clients? Thoroughly review their resumes and conduct reference checks to gather a comprehensive picture of their professional history and character. Reference checks aren't simply about verifying employment dates and job titles; they're an opportunity to gather qualitative data about the candidate's work ethic, interpersonal skills, and overall character.

ASK SPECIFIC QUESTIONS about their work habits, their problem-solving skills, and their interactions with colleagues. Look for consistent themes and patterns in the responses to help you form a well-rounded assessment. Remember, the aim isn't to find perfect individuals, as no one is without flaws. Instead, the goal is to identify candidates who demonstrate a commitment to continuous growth and self-improvement.

During the interview, explore their approaches to personal development. Ask about their learning styles, their willingness to embrace constructive criticism, and their commitment to ongoing professional development. Individuals who consistently seek opportunities for growth and demonstrate a willingness to learn from their mistakes are more likely to align with a faith-based culture of continuous improvement.

The integration of Christian values into the hiring process doesn't necessitate a departure from standard HR practices.

Instead, it enriches the process by adding a layer of

intentional focus on character and values. By thoughtfully crafting interview questions, carefully observing candidate behavior, and thoroughly conducting reference checks, you can build a team that not only excels in its professional capabilities but also embodies the principles of integrity, compassion, and teamwork.

This approach ensures a work environment that is not only productive and profitable but also reflects the positive and empowering influence of faith.

This is more than simply filling a job position; it's about building a community of believers working collaboratively towards a common goal, fostering an environment where faith and work complement each other, leading to increased job satisfaction, employee retention, and overall organizational success.

It's crucial to maintain a balance. While identifying these character traits is essential, remember to comply with all legal requirements regarding employment practices. Avoid discriminatory practices and ensure that your interview questions are job-related and consistent with Equal Employment Opportunity (EEO) guidelines. Focus on observable behaviors and quantifiable achievements,

avoiding inquiries into personal beliefs or practices that are not relevant to the job.

REMEMBER, THE AIM IS to find

individuals who reflect the positive aspects of Christian values in their professional conduct – values that are

beneficial in any work environment, regardless of religious affiliation. Finally, consider incorporating a structured interview process to ensure consistency and fairness. Develop a standardized set of questions that target the key character traits you seek, ensuring each candidate receives the same assessment.

Use a rating scale to objectively evaluate responses and reduce bias in the decision-making

process. This approach not only increases the fairness and accuracy of the hiring process, but also strengthens the overall process, ensuring the consistent application of your organization's values. This also makes it easier to defend your hiring decisions against potential legal challenges, should they arise. By combining thoughtful preparation, ethical considerations, and a focus on the desired character traits, the hiring process becomes an opportunity to strengthen your team and build a work

environment that reflects your values while remaining fully compliant with all legal and ethical requirements. The result is a team that is not only highly skilled and productive but also embodies the positive and transformative power of faith in the workplace, resulting in a more fulfilling and successful work experience for everyone involved. This holistic approach ensures a work environment that thrives on mutual respect, collaboration, and shared purpose, all while remaining grounded in the principles of faith and integrity.

BUILDING A DIVERSE and Inclusive Team

Building a diverse and inclusive team is not merely a matter of ticking boxes to meet legal requirements; it's a reflection of our faith's core tenets of love, acceptance, and the inherent dignity of every individual. As Christians, we are called to see the image of God in each person we encounter, regardless of their background, beliefs, or experiences.

THIS UNDERSTANDING fundamentally shapes our approach to building a team, moving beyond mere compliance to a genuine commitment to fostering a workplace where everyone can flourish.

Our faith teaches us that diversity is not just desirable but essential. It enriches our perspectives, strengthens our problem-solving capabilities, and fosters creativity. A team composed of individuals from diverse cultural, ethnic, and socioeconomic backgrounds brings a wealth of unique experiences and viewpoints to the table.

This diversity enhances our ability to connect with a wider range of clients and customers, understanding their needs and preferences on a deeper level. It allows us to anticipate challenges and opportunities that might otherwise be missed in a homogenous environment. It fosters innovation by

encouraging diverse thought processes and approaches to problem-solving. However, simply hiring individuals from diverse

backgrounds isn't enough to create a truly inclusive

environment.

TRUE INCLUSIVITY REQUIRES a conscious and ongoing effort to ensure that every team member feels valued, respected, and empowered to contribute their unique talents. This involves cultivating a culture of empathy and understanding, where differences are celebrated rather than feared. This requires intentional steps in our hiring process. Our job descriptions should be carefully crafted to attract a broad range of candidates, avoiding language that might unintentionally exclude certain groups.

WE MUST ACTIVELY SEEK out candidates from underrepresented groups, partnering with organizations that focus on diversity and inclusion. Our interview process should be structured to assess not only technical skills and experience but also the candidate's ability to work collaboratively and respectfully within a diverse team. We can use a variety of interview methods - including behavioral interviews to uncover candidates' experiences in collaborative settings and their approach to conflict resolution.

BEYOND THE INITIAL hiring process, building an inclusive workplace requires consistent attention and effort. We need to establish clear policies and procedures that prohibit discrimination and harassment of any kind. These policies should be regularly reviewed and updated to ensure they remain relevant and effective. Moreover, these policies should be more than just words on paper; they must be actively enforced and supported by leadership at every level.

TRANSPARENCY IS CRUCIAL, ensuring everyone understands what constitutes inappropriate behavior and the consequences of such actions. Implementing effective diversity and inclusion training is another vital step. This training shouldn't just be a one-time event, but an ongoing process to raise awareness, challenge biases, and equip our employees with the skills to build a more inclusive workplace. The training should focus on practical skills, including active listening, respectful communication, and conflict resolution.

CRUCIALLY, IT SHOULD focus on fostering empathy, helping team members understand and appreciate different perspectives. Furthermore, we must create opportunities for employees from diverse backgrounds to network and connect with one another. Mentorship programs can pair experienced employees with those newer to the organization, providing guidance and support. Employee resource groups (ERGs) provide a space for employees with shared identities or interests to connect, share experiences, and advocate for their needs.

These groups serve as invaluable resources, fostering a sense of community and belonging. Open and honest communication is the cornerstone of building a diverse and inclusive workplace. Creating channels for feedback is paramount. Regular surveys, focus groups, and one-on-one conversations provide valuable insights into the experiences of our employees. By actively soliciting feedback and responding to concerns, we demonstrate our commitment to creating a truly inclusive environment. This shows a willingness to listen and learn, and to adapt our practices accordingly.

It demonstrates that we value the contributions of every team member. But building an inclusive team doesn't end with policies and training; it requires a fundamental shift in mindset. As Christian leaders, we should strive to embody the qualities of Christ – love, compassion, humility, and forgiveness. These values should guide our interactions with our employees, shaping our decision-making processes and influencing our overall leadership style. It's about building relationships based on mutual respect and

UNDERSTANDING, FOSTERING an environment where every individual feels safe, valued, and empowered to contribute their best. This involves understanding the different cultural norms and communication styles that our team members bring to the workplace. For instance, direct communication that might be common in some cultures may be perceived as aggressive or insensitive in others. We must be mindful of these nuances and strive to communicate in a way that is respectful and inclusive of all cultures represented on our team.

Active listening is key – truly hearing what people are saying and understanding their perspective, rather than just waiting for our turn to speak. This is a crucial element of empathy. Conflict is inevitable in any workplace, but our approach to conflict resolution should be guided by our Christian values. Rather than viewing disagreements as threats, we should view them as opportunities for growth and understanding.

WE SHOULD STRIVE TO address conflict peacefully, seeking to understand the root causes and find solutions that are fair and equitable for all parties involved. Forgiveness should be a central element of our conflict resolution process. Building a diverse and inclusive team requires a long-term commitment, not just a short-term project. It involves ongoing learning, adaptation, and a willingness to continuously improve our practices. We must remain vigilant in our efforts to ensure that our workplace reflects the values of our faith, creating an environment where every individual can thrive and reach their full potential.

This commitment to diversity and inclusion extends beyond simply representing different groups within the company; it must be reflected in leadership roles and decision-making processes. Actively promoting and supporting individuals from diverse backgrounds into leadership positions is a tangible demonstration of our commitment to true inclusivity. It ensures that diverse voices are heard and considered at all levels of the organization, influencing strategy and impacting the overall direction of the company.

THIS NOT ONLY BENEFITS the company, but also acts as an encouragement to other diverse candidates, creating a positive feedback loop. Furthermore, we should strive to create a workplace where employees feel comfortable expressing their faith or beliefs, while respecting the beliefs of others. We need to find a balance where individual expressions of faith are welcomed and celebrated, without imposing those beliefs on others. It's about creating a welcoming and respectful environment where everyone feels safe to be themselves.

This requires careful consideration and a willingness to navigate complex situations with sensitivity and grace. Finally, remember that building a truly diverse and inclusive workplace is a journey, not a destination. It's a continuous process of learning, growing, and adapting. There will inevitably be challenges and setbacks along the way. But by remaining committed to our faith and our values, we can overcome these challenges and create a workplace that is not only successful but also deeply fulfilling and meaningful for all involved.

The result will be a team that is stronger, more innovative, and more reflective of God's love and grace. It is a testament to our commitment to living out our faith in all aspects of our lives, including the workplace. It's a demonstration of how faith can shape our leadership and create a truly positive and impactful working environment. The tangible results are a more engaged workforce, improved productivity, enhanced creativity, and a workplace culture that promotes respect and understanding.

***

ONBOARDING NEW EMPLOYEES with a Focus on Community

Integrating new employees into our team isn't simply about paperwork and introductions; it's about weaving them into the fabric of our community, fostering a sense of belonging that mirrors the love and acceptance we find in our faith.

This approach, rooted in Christian values, transforms onboarding from a mere administrative task into a vital spiritual practice.

We see it as an opportunity to extend the grace and compassion of God to those joining our team, ensuring they feel valued, supported, and empowered from day one. Our onboarding process begins even before the first day. We personalize welcome packages, not just with company information, but with a handwritten note expressing our excitement to have them join us. This small act of personal connection sets the tone for a welcoming and inclusive environment.

WITHIN THE PACKAGE, we might include a small gift reflecting our organizational values – perhaps a book on servant leadership, a donation made in their name to a local charity, or a gift certificate to a nearby coffee shop, encouraging them to connect with the local community. This intentional gesture demonstrates our commitment to them as individuals, extending beyond the purely professional.

The first day itself is meticulously planned to minimize anxiety and maximize engagement. A designated mentor, carefully selected for their empathy and experience, guides the new employee, answering questions, and providing reassurance. This mentor acts as a bridge between the individual and the larger team, fostering a sense of immediate connection and preventing feelings of isolation.

We understand that new beginnings can be daunting; our goal is to create a supportive and nurturing environment where anxieties can be addressed, and questions can be freely asked. The focus is on relationship-building rather than information overload. During the first week, we facilitate opportunities for casual interactions outside formal training sessions. Lunch meetings, coffee breaks, and informal team gatherings create a space for relationship

building. We encourage team members to share personal anecdotes, creating a relaxed atmosphere where newcomers feel comfortable sharing about themselves, building trust and rapport. We believe that a strong foundation of personal connection underpins productivity and team cohesion; this belief translates into intentional time dedicated to fostering these connections.

Our aim isn't just to integrate new employees into workflows; it's to integrate them into our family.

Formal training is incorporated strategically, ensuring that it's interspersed with opportunities for social interaction and team bonding. We believe that knowledge absorption is enhanced when accompanied by a sense of belonging.

We don't bombard new hires with an overwhelming amount of information at once; instead, we adopt a phased approach, ensuring that they can assimilate the information gradually and effectively.

WE ALSO PRIORITIZE experiential learning, allowing new hires to actively participate in projects and contribute to the team's goals from the outset. This provides a sense of ownership and accelerates the integration process. Beyond the initial weeks, we implement ongoing mentorship programs to ensure that new hires continue to receive support and guidance. These programs are designed not just for professional development but also for spiritual growth and personal well-being. We organize regular team-building activities that promote collaboration and camaraderie.

These aren't just corporate events; they're opportunities to deepen relationships, share life experiences, and build a stronger sense of community. This might involve volunteering at a local charity, participating in a community service project, or simply enjoying a casual outing together. Transparency and open communication are central to our approach. We foster a culture of feedback, where employees feel comfortable expressing their thoughts and concerns. This isn't just about addressing operational issues; it's about creating a space where individuals feel heard, valued, and respected. Regular check-ins with mentors, managers, and HR provide a safe platform for feedback and support, allowing us to proactively address any challenges that might arise. This consistent communication ensures that we remain in tune with the needs of everyone, fostering a sense of connectedness that is crucial to a thriving work environment. We also leverage technology to enhance the onboarding experience. We utilize collaborative platforms to facilitate communication, information sharing, and team interaction.

These tools aren't simply for task management; they're
designed to foster a sense of community, allowing
employees to connect and collaborate regardless of their location or working style. We emphasize the use of these platforms to share positive news and celebrate individual and team successes, creating a positive and encouraging atmosphere. Furthermore, we recognize the importance of work-life balance and encourage new employees to establish healthy boundaries from the outset. We promote flexible working arrangements where appropriate, recognizing the importance of personal well-being and family life. This approach demonstrates our commitment to respecting the whole person – professional and personal – reflecting our understanding that a balanced life is essential for both individual and organizational success. This is a critical aspect

of fostering a healthy and sustainable work environment, allowing our team members to thrive, both professionally and personally.

Conflict resolution is another crucial element of our onboarding process.

We proactively equip new employees with conflict resolution skills, teaching them how to navigate disagreements in a constructive and respectful manner. This training emphasizes empathy, understanding, and forgiveness, reflecting our faith-based values. We provide tools and strategies for addressing conflict peacefully and productively, ensuring that disagreements are resolved in a way that strengthens relationships, rather than causing damage.

WE REINFORCE THE IMPORTANCE of seeing the image of God in every individual, even those we might disagree with, encouraging reconciliation and mutual understanding. Finally, we encourage new employees to actively participate in the life of the wider organization. This might include involvement in employee resource groups, social clubs, or community service initiatives. These opportunities provide a sense of purpose and belonging, extending beyond their immediate team.

They're vital in creating a culture of collaboration, support, and shared purpose that fosters deeper connections and strengthens the overall organizational community. It's about demonstrating that we're not just colleagues; we are a community of faith, working together to build something meaningful. The tangible results of this approach are a more engaged workforce, a stronger sense of team unity, and an improved organizational culture that reflects the Christian values we uphold.

Our approach to onboarding is a testament to our belief that building a strong and successful team starts with cultivating a loving and supportive community. It's about recognizing the inherent dignity of everyone, fostering a sense of belonging, and empowering our employees to reach their full potential. This isn't simply a business strategy; it's a reflection of our faith, a living testament to the principles of love, compassion, and grace that guide our lives.

IT'S A JOURNEY OF CONTINUOUS growth and refinement, constantly evolving to best meet the needs of our expanding team and reflecting the ever-deepening understanding of our faith in the workplace. The result is a team that is not only highly productive but also deeply fulfilled and meaningfully connected. The investment in this holistic approach to onboarding yields profound results far exceeding mere efficiency gains; it builds a vibrant, collaborative, and spiritually enriching work environment that reflects the heart of our faith.

This approach ultimately fosters loyalty, increases retention rates, and strengthens the overall moral compass of the organization. It's a testament to the transformative power of faith in the workplace, demonstrating how Christian values can create a truly exceptional and successful team. We actively seek feedback from new employees throughout the onboarding process, ensuring our strategies remain relevant and effective in fostering a positive and inclusive community. This constant evaluation and adaptation allow us to continuously improve and refine our approach, ensuring that each new employee feels valued, supported, and integrated into our team from day one. The long-term benefits are invaluable, contributing to a stronger, more cohesive, and ultimately, more successful organization. **Mentoring and Developing Employees Spiritually Optional**

The question of offering spiritual guidance in the workplace, particularly within a Christian context, requires careful consideration.

OUR COMMITMENT TO CREATING a welcoming and inclusive environment for all employees, regardless of their faith or belief system, is paramount. While we strive to foster a workplace culture reflecting our Christian values –emphasizing compassion, integrity, and servant leadership –we understand that not everyone shares our faith. Therefore, any form of spiritual mentoring or development must be entirely voluntary and offered with utmost sensitivity and respect for individual beliefs.

Our approach focuses on creating opportunities for personal and professional growth that resonate with a diverse workforce. We offer a range of development programs that address various aspects of employee well-being, including leadership training, communication skills workshops, and stress management seminars. These programs are designed to equip employees with the tools they need to excel in their roles and contribute to the overall success of the organization.

WE BELIEVE THAT FOSTERING a strong sense of community, built on mutual respect and understanding, is essential for creating a positive and productive work

environment. This community, grounded in the principles of Christian love, naturally provides support and encouragement, which can be a powerful catalyst for

personal and spiritual growth. We recognize that for some employees, their faith plays a significant role in their lives and informs their approach to work.

For those who desire it, we offer opportunities for informal mentorship and spiritual discussion. This might involve pairing an employee with a colleague who shares similar faith-based values, but only if both individuals are comfortable and actively seek such a connection. This isn't a formal program, but rather an organic process facilitated by a strong sense of community and mutual trust. The emphasis remains on fostering authentic relationships built on respect and understanding.

WE CAREFULLY AVOID creating situations where employees might feel pressured or coerced into participating in faith-based activities. A crucial element in this process is ensuring transparency and clarity. We clearly communicate our organizational values and commitment to inclusivity in our employee handbook and during the onboarding process. This communication emphasizes our dedication to respecting individual beliefs and creating a workplace where everyone feels safe, valued, and

RESPECTED, REGARDLESS of their faith or background. We explicitly state that participation in any spiritual mentoring or discussion is entirely voluntary and that no employee will face any adverse consequences for choosing not to participate. This clear communication is vital for maintaining trust and ensuring that our approach to employee development aligns with legal and ethical standards.

WE REGULARLY REVIEW our policies and practices to ensure they continue to uphold our commitment to inclusivity and respect.

We gather feedback from employees through various channels, including employee surveys, focus groups, and regular one-on-one meetings with managers. This feedback mechanism is crucial for identifying areas for improvement and ensuring that our efforts are truly effective in creating a supportive and welcoming environment for all.

To illustrate the practical application of our principles, consider the example of Sarah, a senior project manager who expressed an interest in exploring leadership principles through a faith-based lens.

We connected Sarah with John, another senior leader who also identifies as a Christian.

Their mentorship relationship organically developed, with John sharing his experiences integrating faith into his leadership style and offering guidance based on biblical principles.

HOWEVER, THE FOCUS remained on practical leadership skills and strategies applicable to any workplace context, avoiding overtly religious teachings.

This approach ensures that the mentoring provides professional development alongside spiritual enrichment, catering to the individual's specific needs and interests. The success of this model depends on a delicate balance between fostering a faith-affirming environment and respecting the diverse beliefs of our employees.

We provide regular training to our managers on inclusive leadership practices, focusing on the critical skills of active listening, empathy, and

fostering a safe space for open and respectful dialogue. This training equips our managers to navigate sensitive situations with professionalism and care, while cultivating a supportive environment where employees feel empowered to share their needs and concerns, irrespective of their religious beliefs. Furthermore, our internal communication strategy plays a vital role in reinforcing our commitment to diversity and inclusion.

We regularly share articles and resources that highlight the importance of respecting

different perspectives and creating a welcoming work environment for individuals from all backgrounds. These initiatives contribute to a positive organizational culture that embraces diversity and celebrates individual differences. One potential area of concern is the potential for bias in the workplace. To mitigate this risk, we actively work to promote a diverse leadership team, ensuring that individuals from various

backgrounds are represented in decision-making roles. This diversity enhances perspectives and promotes fairer decision-making processes, minimizing the potential for bias to affect our hiring and promotion practices. Our commitment to fostering a spiritually enriching workplace is not about imposing religious beliefs; rather, it's about integrating the positive values of our faith into the fabric of our organizational culture. It's about extending compassion, practicing forgiveness, promoting integrity, and cultivating a sense of community based on mutual respect and understanding.

It's about fostering an environment where everyone feels valued and empowered to reach their full potential, both personally and professionally. We acknowledge that this approach requires ongoing

vigilance and refinement. The evolving landscape of the workplace necessitates a continuous evaluation of our

practices to ensure that they remain appropriate and

respectful. We engage in regular dialogue with employees and seek external guidance from legal and ethical experts to ensure we meet the highest standards of workplace inclusivity and legality. The integration of faith into our workplace isn't about proselytizing; it's about embodying the principles of love, compassion, and forgiveness in our daily interactions. It's about creating an environment of mutual support and

encouragement, where employees feel safe, respected, and empowered to bring their whole selves to work. This holistic approach, focusing on both professional and spiritual well-being, results in a more engaged, productive, and ultimately more successful workforce. It's a testament to the power of integrating positive values into the workplace, demonstrating that faith and professional success are not mutually exclusive but can instead complement and enhance each other,

fostering a thriving and fulfilling work environment. Our approach to spiritual development, therefore, is less about formal programs and more about cultivating a culture where these values naturally emerge.

We recognize that the specific ways in which these values manifest will vary depending on individual experiences and beliefs. We prioritize creating a supportive and understanding environment where employees feel comfortable exploring their faith (or lack thereof) in their own way, without feeling pressured or judged. This subtle yet significant approach allows us to cultivate a workplace that is both productive and spiritually resonant for many, while remaining fully inclusive of everyone.

We regularly conduct anonymous surveys to gauge employee satisfaction and identify areas for improvement in our diversity and inclusion initiatives. This continuous feedback loop allows us to adjust our strategies, ensuring that our efforts effectively support all employees, regardless of their backgrounds or beliefs. This process is not static; it's a dynamic process of ongoing review and refinement, adapting to the changing needs and expectations of our ever-growing workforce.

THE GOAL IS ALWAYS to create an environment where every employee feels valued, respected, and empowered to contribute their unique talents and perspectives, fostering a thriving and inclusive workplace that reflects the best aspects of our shared humanity. Our commitment to this endeavor is unwavering, guided by a deep belief in the inherent worth and dignity of each individual.

THE POWER OF EMPATHY in Conflict Resolution

Empathy, the ability to understand and share the feelings of another, is not merely a soft skill; it's a powerful tool in conflict resolution. In my years as an HR professional, guided by my Christian faith, I've witnessed firsthand how empathy transforms tense situations into opportunities for growth and reconciliation. It's about stepping into someone else's shoes, seeing the world from their perspective, and acknowledging their emotions, even if you don't agree with their actions or viewpoints. This isn't about condoning wrongdoing, but about understanding the root causes of conflict. Often, anger, resentment, and frustration stem from unmet needs, feelings of injustice, or perceived slights. By actively listening and seeking to understand these underlying emotions, we can begin to bridge the gap and find common ground. For example, I once faced a conflict between two team leaders – Sarah and Mark – who were locked in a bitter dispute over project allocation. Each felt their project was more important, and their arguments became increasingly personal. Instead of immediately intervening and assigning blame, I took a step back and individually spoke with both Sarah and Mark.

During these conversations, I focused on actively listening, allowing them to express their frustrations and concerns without interruption. I asked open-ended questions designed to uncover the underlying emotional drivers of their conflict: "Sarah, can you tell me more about why you feel this project is so crucial?" or "Mark, what are your concerns about the impact of this allocation decision on your team's morale?" Through this process of empathetic listening, I discovered that Sarah's intense advocacy stemmed from a fear of her team missing a critical deadline, which could jeopardize their bonus. Mark, on the other hand, felt his team was unfairly burdened, leading to feelings of resentment and exhaustion. Neither was inherently malicious; their actions stemmed from legitimate concerns. This understanding was crucial in transforming the conflict.

Once I grasped the emotional core of their disagreement, I could facilitate a more productive conversation. I reframed the problem, focusing not on assigning blame, but on finding a solution that addressed the needs of both teams. We collaboratively brainstormed solutions, considering things like re-allocating tasks, extending deadlines, or providing additional resources to Mark's team. The key was to involve both parties in the solution-finding process, empowering them to feel heard and valued.

This approach, rooted in empathy, ultimately led to a

resolution that satisfied both Sarah and Mark. They not only resolved their immediate conflict but also developed a greater appreciation for each other's perspectives. They learned to communicate more effectively, recognizing the importance of voicing concerns and collaborating toward mutually beneficial outcomes. The experience strengthened their working relationship and fostered a more positive team dynamic.

THE POWER OF EMPATHY lies not just in resolving individual conflicts but in building a culture of understanding and mutual respect within the workplace. The principle of empathy extends beyond resolving major conflicts. It's equally vital in addressing smaller disagreements and everyday workplace interactions. A simple act of acknowledging someone's frustration, even with a brief "I understand this is frustrating for you," can significantly de-escalate a tense situation.

Similarly, taking the time to listen actively, without judgment, can build trust and rapport, making people feel heard and respected. This creates a safer environment where employees feel

comfortable expressing concerns without fear of reprisal or misunderstanding. In my experience, fostering a culture of empathy involves modeling the behavior myself. This means being vulnerable, admitting when I've made mistakes, and demonstrating genuine care for my employees' well-being.

It also involves creating opportunities for team members to connect on a personal level, allowing them to develop empathy for each other through shared experiences and understanding. Team-building activities, informal gatherings, and open communication channels are all essential elements in cultivating this type of empathetic environment. Moreover, I've found that incorporating my Christian faith strengthens my ability to practice empathy. The biblical principles of love, compassion, and forgiveness provide a strong ethical framework for resolving conflicts. The emphasis on understanding and forgiving others, regardless of their actions, deeply informs my approach to conflict resolution. I strive to see each person as a valuable individual, created in God's image, deserving of respect and understanding, even when they are in the wrong. This belief system guides my interactions and enables me to approach conflicts with patience, grace, and a genuine desire to help others.

Beyond the immediate resolution of conflict, a culture rooted in empathy yields long-term benefits for the organization. Employees who feel understood, valued, and respected are more engaged, productive, and loyal. They are more likely to go the extra mile, contribute creatively, and remain committed to the organization's success. Reduced turnover, increased morale, and improved overall productivity are all tangible outcomes of fostering a workplace where empathy is valued and practiced. This positive feedback loop creates a virtuous cycle, where empathy leads to positive outcomes, further reinforcing its importance within the organizational culture. However, practicing empathy effectively requires a delicate balance. While it's essential to understand and acknowledge the emotions of others, it's equally important to maintain professional boundaries. Empathy doesn't mean condoning harmful behavior or compromising organizational values. It means understanding the underlying reasons behind

behavior, providing support and guidance, while still holding individuals accountable for their actions. This requires careful discernment and a commitment to upholding ethical standards. One specific example involved a particularly challenging situation with an employee, David, who consistently missed deadlines and failed to meet performance expectations. Initially, I might have been inclined to focus solely on the negative consequences of his actions – the missed deadlines, the frustrated colleagues, the potential impact on projects.

However, applying empathy shifted my focus. I took the time to understand the underlying reasons behind his poor performance. Through empathetic conversations, I discovered that David was struggling with significant personal issues outside of work – family problems and health concerns – that heavily impacted his ability to concentrate and meet deadlines. Understanding this context allowed me to approach the situation differently. Instead of solely focusing on disciplinary action, I worked with David to develop a personalized performance improvement plan that addressed both his work-related challenges and personal struggles. We explored flexible work arrangements, provided additional support, and connected him with employee assistance resources. This empathetic approach not only helped David improve his performance but also fostered a stronger, more trusting relationship between us. He felt heard, understood, and supported, which fostered a more collaborative approach to problem-solving. His performance improved significantly, and he became a more engaged and valuable member of the team.

This demonstrates that even in situations where

performance issues exist, empathy plays a crucial role in achieving positive outcomes. In conclusion, the power of empathy in conflict resolution is undeniable. It transforms tense situations into opportunities for growth, understanding, and reconciliation. By cultivating a culture of empathy, organizations can build stronger, more engaged teams, fostering a workplace where individuals feel valued, supported, and respected. This creates a positive feedback loop, leading to higher productivity, improved morale, and greater success for both the individuals and the organization. And as a Christian leader, I see this approach as a powerful reflection of the love, compassion, and forgiveness central to my faith. It's not merely a professional strategy; it's a fundamental aspect of how I strive to lead and serve.

Addressing Difficult Conversations with Grace and Truth

Addressing difficult conversations is an inevitable part of leadership, particularly in HR. However, approaching these conversations with grace and truth, while maintaining a strong Christian foundation, can transform them from potential sources of conflict into opportunities for growth and reconciliation. My faith has profoundly shaped my approach, emphasizing empathy, forgiveness, and a focus on restorative justice rather than retribution. This isn't about avoiding accountability; it's about pursuing it with compassion and understanding. One recurring challenge I've faced is addressing performance issues. Instead of launching into criticism, I've learned to preface the conversation with prayer, seeking God's guidance and wisdom. This centers me and allows me to approach the employee with a spirit of genuine care, rather than judgment. I start by affirming their value and contributions to the team, acknowledging their positive attributes before addressing areas for improvement.

For example, instead of saying, "Your performance has been unacceptable," I might say, "I've noticed some challenges in meeting certain deadlines lately, and I want to work with you to find solutions." This subtle shift in language dramatically alters the tone of the conversation. It avoids the immediate defensiveness that blunt criticism can trigger. It's crucial to listen actively, allowing the employee to share their perspective. Perhaps there are underlying issues—personal struggles, family problems, or even workplace stressors—that are affecting their performance. These are not excuses, but they are crucial pieces of the puzzle. Listening empathetically allows me to understand the context, offering support and potential solutions, rather than simply imposing corrective actions. Furthermore, I find the principles of restorative justice

deeply helpful. Instead of focusing solely on punishment, I strive to repair the harm caused by the performance issue and restore the relationship between the employee and the team. This might involve creating a performance improvement plan with specific, measurable, achievable, relevant, and time-bound (SMART) goals. Regular check-ins become a critical part of this process, demonstrating ongoing support and a commitment to the employee's growth. These meetings aren't just about evaluating progress; they're about fostering a partnership in improving performance. They offer a safe space for open communication and a chance to adjust the plan as needed. Another challenging scenario involves mediating conflicts between employees. My Christian faith compels me to approach such situations with a focus on reconciliation.

I believe that forgiveness is not just a personal virtue but a crucial element of building a healthy and productive workplace. However, forgiveness doesn't mean condoning unacceptable behavior. It means choosing to release resentment and bitterness, creating space for healing and restoring relationships. Before mediating a conflict, I pray for wisdom and discernment, asking God to guide my words and actions. This prayer isn't about seeking a specific outcome but about aligning my intentions with his principles of love, justice, and mercy.

Mediation sessions begin by creating a safe and respectful environment. Each party is given an opportunity to share their perspective without interruption. Active listening is paramount. I strive to understand the root causes of the conflict, not just the surface-level disagreements. Often, misunderstandings or miscommunications are at the heart of the issue. Once both parties feel heard and understood, I guide them towards finding a mutually acceptable solution. This process often involves compromise and a willingness to forgive.

I emphasize the importance of focusing on the future rather than dwelling on past hurts. Forgiveness, in this context, isn't about forgetting; it's about choosing to let go of anger and resentment, opening the way for reconciliation and healing. Sometimes, a formal agreement, outlining specific steps for moving forward, is helpful. It provides a framework for restoring positive working relationships and prevents future conflicts from arising. This agreement should not be punitive but restorative, focused on repairing relationships and creating a more positive work environment. Even addressing sensitive issues like harassment or discrimination requires navigating this delicate balance of grace and truth. My approach, rooted in my faith, doesn't compromise on accountability. However, it emphasizes compassion and empathy. Investigating such allegations requires sensitivity and fairness. The goal isn't to punish, but to ensure a safe and inclusive environment for all employees. This requires a thorough and impartial investigation, involving careful consideration of all evidence.

It's critical to maintain confidentiality throughout the process, protecting the rights and privacy of all involved. The outcome should be just and equitable, promoting healing and preventing future incidents. In cases of harassment, for instance, the focus shifts to restoring trust and ensuring a safe work environment. This might involve mandatory training, disciplinary action (depending on the severity), and individual counseling for both the victim and the perpetrator. Ultimately, the goal is not just to address the specific incident but to create a culture where such behavior is unacceptable and where individuals feel empowered to report incidents without fear of retaliation. Addressing difficult conversations is not an easy task, but it is a critical aspect of effective leadership. My faith profoundly influences my approach, allowing me to handle these challenges with both grace and truth. By combining Christian principles of forgiveness, empathy, and restorative justice with practical HR strategies, I have found it possible to transform these potentially divisive situations into opportunities for growth, reconciliation, and the strengthening of team cohesion. This commitment to both faith and professional excellence is not merely a personal choice; it is integral to my leadership style, creating a positive and productive work environment for everyone. It reflects a leadership style built upon love, understanding, and a commitment to fostering a community where every individual feels valued and respected. The process often involves a delicate balance. While being firm and upholding company policies, I find it crucial to approach each situation with an understanding heart, remembering that every individual is created in God's image and deserves respect and dignity. It's about seeing the human being behind the performance issue, the conflict, or the wrongdoing. This holistic perspective, shaped by my faith, allows me to address issues with both firmness and compassion, leading to more effective and lasting resolutions. Further, it's important to remember that these difficult conversations are often emotionally taxing for both the leader and the employee.

SELF-CARE IS CRUCIAL. After each challenging conversation, I often take time to debrief, reflecting on my actions and seeking guidance through prayer. This process helps me process my emotions and ensures that I am equipped to handle future situations with renewed compassion and energy. It's not just about managing employees; it's about caring for them, guiding them, and supporting their growth, both professionally and personally. This holistic approach, firmly rooted in my Christian faith, forms the cornerstone of my leadership philosophy.

Finally, it's essential to document these conversations thoroughly and ethically. This documentation serves as a record of events, the decisions made, and the actions taken. It protects both the employee and the organization. However, it is crucial to handle this documentation with sensitivity and respect, always remembering that this

information is confidential and should be treated with the utmost care. This adherence to ethical practices reinforces the trust and respect that are central to building a positive and productive work environment.

My faith guides me to maintain integrity and transparency in all my actions, ensuring that the processes are fair, just, and compassionate. In essence, integrating faith-based principles into the realm of difficult conversations not only provides a moral compass but also leads to more effective conflict resolution and a more harmonious workplace.

Creating a Culture of Open Communication

Building a culture of open communication is paramount to fostering a truly caring and supportive work environment. It's more than just encouraging employees to talk; it's about creating a safe space where honest dialogue flourishes, where concerns are voiced without fear of retribution, and where feedback, both positive and constructive, is freely exchanged. This, I believe, is a direct reflection of God's love – a love that is open, accepting, and forgiving. In my experience leading teams that have grown from 500 to 2500 employees, I've learned that creating this kind of

environment requires consistent effort, a deliberate strategy, and a deep commitment to empathy. One key element is establishing clear and consistent

communication channels. This goes beyond simply having regular team meetings; it involves multiple avenues for communication that cater to different preferences and needs. For instance, we implemented a robust intranet system with easily accessible information, a dedicated forum for questions and discussions, and even a suggestion box – both digital and physical – where employees could anonymously share their thoughts and ideas. This multi-faceted approach ensures that everyone has a voice and feels heard, regardless of their communication style or comfort level. We also established regular one-on-one meetings between managers and their team members, creating a space for open and honest conversations, fostering a personal connection vital for building trust and understanding. Transparency is equally crucial.

Employees need to understand the "why" behind decisions, even the difficult ones.

Keeping them informed, even when the news isn't positive, demonstrates respect and builds trust. During periods of organizational change, for example, we prioritized regular updates and town hall meetings to address concerns, answer questions, and quell anxieties. This open communication not only minimized rumors and misunderstandings but also fostered a sense of shared responsibility and collective ownership. This aligns with the biblical principle of accountability, ensuring everyone understands their role and contribution to the overall success of the organization. Furthermore, actively soliciting feedback is essential. We implemented 360-degree feedback systems, anonymous surveys, and regular pulse checks to gauge employee

sentiment and identify areas for improvement. This approach provided valuable insights into employee satisfaction, morale, and productivity. Analyzing this data allowed us to identify recurring concerns, address systemic issues, and implement targeted solutions.

Critically, we ensured that feedback mechanisms were anonymous to create a genuinely safe space for honest input. This resonates with the Christian value of humility, recognizing that we are not always perfect, and that continuous improvement is an essential part of our journey. Encouraging upward communication is just as critical as downward communication.

We implemented mechanisms to encourage employees to directly share their ideas, concerns, and suggestions with upper management, bypassing unnecessary layers of bureaucracy. This was facilitated through open-door policies, regular suggestion boxes, and designated channels for voicing concerns. These channels provided avenues for addressing problems before they escalated into major conflicts, promoting a proactive and preventative approach to conflict resolution.

THIS FOSTERS A SENSE of ownership and empowers employees, reminding them that their voices matter and are valued within the organization. However, open communication isn't just about systems and structures; it's fundamentally about fostering a culture of trust and respect. This requires a conscious effort from every level of leadership, starting from the top. Leaders must model the behavior they expect from their team members.

THIS MEANS ACTIVELY listening, being receptive to criticism, and demonstrating a willingness to engage in difficult conversations. It's about creating a space where vulnerability is accepted, mistakes are seen as learning opportunities, and forgiveness is extended freely. Leading by example is key. When leaders demonstrate openness and honesty in their own communication, it creates a ripple effect throughout the organization.

For instance, I have always strived to be transparent about my own struggles and challenges, both professionally and personally. This vulnerability has not only built stronger relationships with my team but has also fostered a culture of mutual support and understanding. Sharing personal experiences, especially those reflecting faith, has created deeper connections and fostered a sense of shared humanity.

This approach resonates with the Christian principle of humility, acknowledging our imperfections and relying on God's grace. Active listening is another crucial skill for fostering open communication. It's not enough to simply hear what someone is saying, it's vital to understand their perspective, empathize with their feelings, and respond in a way that shows genuine care and concern. This involves paying close attention to both verbal and nonverbal cues, asking clarifying questions, summarizing their points to ensure understanding, and reflecting on their feelings to demonstrate empathy. This deep listening creates a safe space for employees to share their honest thoughts and feelings, knowing they are truly heard and understood. This practice is rooted in Christian values of love and compassion, emphasizing the importance of seeing every individual as a unique and valuable creation of God. Furthermore, providing regular and constructive feedback is essential for fostering a culture of continuous improvement. This means providing regular feedback on performance, both positive and negative, in a timely and constructive manner.

WE IMPLEMENTED A SYSTEM of regular performance reviews and informal check-ins, offering specific examples of strengths and areas for improvement. Critically, we ensured that feedback was delivered with empathy and a focus on growth, avoiding judgmental or critical language. This approach mirrors the biblical principle of grace and mercy, acknowledging human imperfections and focusing on individual growth. Conflict resolution is an inevitable part of any team dynamic.

HOWEVER, OPEN COMMUNICATION can significantly help in managing and resolving conflicts effectively. When conflicts arise, it's crucial to create a safe and structured environment where employees feel comfortable expressing their concerns and finding mutually acceptable solutions. We developed a clear conflict resolution process, incorporating elements of restorative justice, focusing on reconciliation and healing rather than retribution.

THIS APPROACH REFLECTS the Christian values of forgiveness and reconciliation, promoting healing and rebuilding trust within the team. Finally, maintaining confidentiality is paramount in creating a culture of open communication. Employees must trust that their concerns and personal information will be handled with respect and discretion. Establishing clear guidelines and procedures for handling sensitive information is crucial.

THIS INCLUDES ADHERING to relevant data protection regulations and clearly outlining the boundaries of confidentiality. This ethical approach is a crucial aspect of building trust and fostering a safe space for open dialogue, mirroring the Christian value of discretion and maintaining the privacy of individuals. In conclusion, building a culture of open communication is a continuous journey, not a destination. It requires consistent effort, deliberate strategies, and a genuine commitment to creating a supportive and caring environment where every individual feels valued, respected, and heard.

By integrating Christian values of love, compassion, empathy, and forgiveness into our communication practices, we can create workplaces that are not only productive but also profoundly humanizing and life-giving, reflecting God's love in action. This approach has been instrumental in my leadership journey, helping me build and manage teams' of 2500 employees with a strong sense of unity and purpose. It's a testament to the power of integrating faith into professional life, leading to a more harmonious and fulfilling work experience for everyone involved.

Providing Support and Encouragement to Employees

Building upon the foundation of open communication, providing tangible support and encouragement is crucial for nurturing a culture of care.

This isn't merely about offering platitudes; it's about demonstrating genuine concern for employees' well-being—both professionally and personally—in practical and meaningful ways.

My faith has taught me that caring for others is an act of worship, a reflection of God's love and compassion. This belief has shaped my approach to leadership, guiding my decisions and actions in ways that create a supportive and encouraging work

environment. One key aspect is actively listening to employees' concerns.

This goes beyond simply hearing their words; it involves understanding their underlying emotions and perspectives.

OFTEN, AN EMPLOYEE'S frustration stems not just from a specific problem but from a deeper sense of feeling unheard or undervalued. Taking the time to truly listen, to show empathy and understanding, can be incredibly powerful. I recall an instance where a team member, burdened by personal challenges outside of work, was struggling to meet deadlines.

Instead of focusing solely on the missed deadlines, I took the time to listen to her concerns, offering not just words of encouragement but also

practical assistance—helping her reorganize her workload, connecting her with resources, and even offering to cover some of her tasks. The result was not just improved performance, but a strengthened relationship built on trust and mutual respect. Beyond active listening, providing practical support is equally vital. This might involve offering flexible work arrangements to accommodate personal needs, providing access to employee assistance programs (EAPs) to address mental health concerns, or offering financial assistance through hardship funds or other programs. Creating a supportive environment also includes fostering a culture of mentorship and peer support. Pairing experienced employees with newer ones can provide invaluable guidance and support, accelerating their professional growth and fostering a sense of belonging. We implemented a robust mentoring program within our company, pairing mentors and mentees based on shared interests and skillsets, resulting in a significant increase in employee engagement and retention. The mentorship program also fostered a sense of community within the company. Furthermore, recognizing and celebrating employees' accomplishments is essential for boosting morale and fostering a sense of appreciation. Public acknowledgments, small tokens of appreciation, and opportunities for professional development all contribute to creating a positive and encouraging work environment.

I strongly believe in celebrating both individual and team successes. We regularly host company-wide events to acknowledge outstanding achievements, creating opportunities for employees to connect and build camaraderie. This, in essence, is mirroring God's celebration of our accomplishments and His rejoicing in our successes. A simple "thank you" can go a long way in showing appreciation for someone's hard work and dedication. However, providing support and encouragement goes beyond tangible actions; it also

encompasses emotional support. This is where my faith has played a particularly significant role. I've learned that sometimes, employees simply need someone to listen without judgment, to offer a comforting presence during challenging times. This can be as simple as offering a listening ear, providing a shoulder to cry on, or offering a prayer. It's crucial to create a space where employees feel safe to be vulnerable and to express their emotions without fear of being judged or ostracized.

My Christian faith teaches me the importance of

compassion, empathy, and unconditional love. I strive to reflect these values in my interactions with employees, treating everyone with dignity and respect.

In leading teams that have grown from 500 to over 2500 employees, I've witnessed firsthand the power of creating a culture of care. This didn't happen overnight; it required a consistent and intentional effort to integrate these principles into our company culture.

It involved educating managers on the importance of empathy and actively listening to employees, providing them with the tools and resources they need to support their teams.

We implemented training programs focusing on active listening, conflict resolution, and emotional intelligence. These programs not only benefited employees but also enhanced managers' leadership skills, enabling them to better support and guide their teams. The outcomes have been remarkable.

We've seen significant improvements in employee engagement, job satisfaction, and retention rates. Providing support also extends to addressing challenging situations with compassion and understanding. Conflicts are inevitable in any workplace, but how we address them significantly impacts the overall work environment. My faith guides me to approach conflict resolution with a spirit of forgiveness and reconciliation. This means avoiding judgmental language, focusing on understanding the perspectives of all parties involved, and striving to find solutions that are fair and equitable. Mediation, rather than confrontation, is crucial in resolving disputes, enabling employees to air their grievances in a safe and respectful manner. We implemented a structured conflict resolution process involving clear guidelines and trained mediators, ensuring that conflicts are addressed promptly and effectively. In managing employees, recognizing their individual

differences is paramount. Each individual is unique, with diverse backgrounds, experiences, and needs.

Understanding these differences is key to providing appropriate support. For instance, some employees may thrive in a fast-paced environment, while others may prefer a more structured and predictable setting. Recognizing these preferences is vital for assigning tasks and providing support that caters to individual needs. Flexible work arrangements, such as telecommuting or adjusted work hours, can significantly contribute to employee well-being and productivity.

BY ACCOMMODATING INDIVIDUAL needs, we can create a work environment that feels inclusive and supportive. Furthermore, ensuring work-life balance is a critical element of fostering a caring work environment. Overwork and burnout are serious concerns, and it's our responsibility to create a culture that encourages employees to prioritize their well-being. Promoting healthy boundaries between work and personal life, encouraging employees to utilize their vacation time, and actively discouraging overworking are essential steps in this direction. We implemented policies that actively encourage employees to disconnect after work hours, fostering a healthy work-life balance that minimizes burnout. Regular wellness initiatives such as employee wellness programs or mental health awareness campaigns are equally vital. These initiatives not only demonstrate a genuine concern for employees' well-being but also promote a healthy and productive work environment.

In conclusion, providing support and encouragement to employees is not merely a managerial function; it is an

integral part of creating a truly caring and supportive

workplace, a reflection of God's love in action. It's about creating a space where employees feel valued, respected, heard, and supported, both professionally and personally. By consistently integrating these principles into our leadership approach, we can foster a workplace where employees thrive, not just as professionals but also as individuals. The rewards are significant—increased employee engagement, higher retention rates, improved productivity, and a strong sense of community—all contributing to a thriving and fulfilling work environment.

This journey of providing support and fostering a culture of care is an ongoing process, requiring continuous learning, adaptation, and a genuine commitment to valuing each member of the team. It's a reflection of my faith in action, a constant reminder that leading with empathy is not just good business practice but a testament to my Christian values.

Maintaining Integrity in the Face of Pressure

The pressure to compromise one's integrity in the workplace is a pervasive reality. As an HR professional, you're often caught in the crosshairs of conflicting demands: pleasing upper management, meeting deadlines, and ensuring employee satisfaction. These pressures can be immense, particularly when navigating complex situations involving employee performance, budget constraints, or legal compliance.

But as a Christian leader, maintaining integrity—adhering to principles of honesty, fairness, and justice—remains paramount. This isn't merely about avoiding legal trouble; it's about upholding the moral compass instilled by your faith. Consider the scenario of budget cuts.

Your organization may mandate layoffs, and you, as the HR leader, are tasked with determining who will be let go. The pressure to choose based on favoritism, or to protect certain individuals regardless of their performance, can be overwhelming. However, applying Christian principles demands a fair and transparent process. This might involve prioritizing objective criteria like performance evaluations, attendance records, and skill sets, ensuring that the decision is devoid of personal biases. This approach, while challenging, demonstrates both professional competence and adherence to your faith's values. Furthermore, it builds trust and respect within the team, even amidst difficult circumstances.

Open communication throughout the process, explaining the criteria used and the rationale behind the decisions, helps mitigate any negative perceptions and fosters understanding. Transparency, fueled by a commitment to fairness, can turn a potentially devastating situation into an opportunity to demonstrate Christian character. Another common challenge arises in situations involving difficult employees. Perhaps an employee consistently violates company policy or displays unprofessional conduct. The temptation to overlook minor infractions or to shy away from confronting the problem can be considerable. However, ignoring such behavior undermines the integrity of the workplace and allows the problem to fester. A Christian leader would approach this situation by employing restorative justice principles. Instead of resorting to immediate disciplinary action, they'd strive to understand the root cause of the employee's behavior, creating an environment of grace and understanding. This approach might involve open and honest conversations with the employee, offering support and guidance while enforcing accountability.

It's about recognizing the inherent worth of each individual while upholding the standards of the organization. The goal is not punishment but correction and restoration, aligning with biblical principles of forgiveness and reconciliation. This approach, while demanding more time and effort, often yields better long-term results, fostering a healthier and more productive work environment.

The pressure to meet unrealistic deadlines or targets can also lead to ethical compromises. The temptation to cut corners, manipulate data, or prioritize speed over quality becomes strong. Yet, maintaining integrity means resisting these temptations. A commitment to quality, even under pressure, is a testimony to both professional competence and Christian character. It's about upholding honesty and transparency in reporting results and avoiding actions that could compromise the organization's reputation or harm employees.

This might require communicating the limitations to upper management, explaining the potential risks associated with pursuing unrealistic goals, and advocating for a more realistic and sustainable approach. This requires courage and conviction, but it's a crucial aspect of maintaining integrity. It's a testament to your commitment to ethical practices and reflects your faith in action. Moreover, the integration of faith into ethical decision-making offers a unique perspective. The Golden Rule—treating others as you would like to be treated—serves as an invaluable guide in navigating complex situations. Before making any decision, ask yourself how your actions would affect the individuals involved.

Would it be fair, just, and compassionate? This principle extends beyond simple interactions and guides the development of policies and procedures.

Consider, for example, the development of a new leave policy. Consulting with employees, soliciting their input, and considering their needs before formulating a policy demonstrates a commitment to fairness and inclusion. It's about creating policies that reflect your belief in the inherent dignity of every employee and support their overall well-being.

This is more than just good HR; it's a reflection of Christian values in action, fostering a more just and equitable work environment. Another critical area where integrity is tested is in maintaining confidentiality and protecting employee privacy. Access to sensitive personal information is a significant responsibility, and the temptation to misuse or divulge such information can be strong.

A Christian leader must approach this with the utmost care, upholding the confidentiality entrusted to them.

This involves strictly adhering to company policies, relevant laws, and ethical principles, while also exercising discretion in personal conversations.

Remember that trust is a cornerstone of any healthy work relationship and sharing confidential information, even seemingly innocuous details, can damage that trust.

This commitment to privacy extends beyond simply complying with regulations; it's about demonstrating respect for the dignity and privacy of every individual.

IT ALIGNS WITH CHRISTIAN principles of love and compassion and contributes to a work environment where trust flourishes. Beyond individual decisions, building a culture of integrity within the entire organization is crucial. This requires setting clear expectations regarding ethical behavior, providing appropriate training and education, and establishing robust reporting mechanisms for addressing ethical concerns. Regular communication about ethical standards and their application within specific work scenarios ensures that all employees understand the importance of integrity and know how to navigate situations where ethical compromises may be tempting. The organization's commitment to ethical conduct must be clearly communicated and consistently enforced, from the top down.

This creates a work environment where integrity isn't just expected, but actively cultivated and celebrated. This holistic approach establishes a strong foundation for the organization's long-term success and ensures that its reputation remains untarnished. Ultimately, maintaining integrity in the face of pressure isn't just about adhering to a set of rules; it's about embodying the values instilled by your faith. It's about consistently demonstrating honesty, fairness, compassion, and justice in all interactions and decisions.

It requires courage, discernment, and a commitment to upholding the highest ethical standards, even when it's difficult. By applying Christian principles in your daily work, you create a workplace that reflects your values, fosters trust, and inspires others to do the same. It's a testament to your faith, and a demonstration of the transformative power of living out your beliefs in your professional life. This commitment will not only elevate your own leadership but will create a more just and

compassionate workplace for everyone. The rewards may not always be immediate or easily quantifiable, but the long-term impact on individuals, teams, and the organization as a whole will be profound and enduring. The legacy of a leader who consistently prioritizes integrity will far outlast any short-term pressures or challenges.

Addressing Workplace Discrimination and Bias

Building a truly inclusive and equitable workplace, one that reflects the inherent dignity and worth of every individual created in God's image, requires a proactive and multifaceted approach. Ignoring or downplaying instances of discrimination and bias, even subtle ones, is not an option for a Christian leader. Silence, in this context, equates to complicity. Our faith calls us to actively combat injustice and champion the cause of the marginalized. This means fostering an environment where individuals feel safe to report discriminatory behavior without fear of reprisal, and where such reports are met with swift, just, and compassionate responses.

One crucial step is establishing clear and comprehensive anti-discrimination policies. These policies shouldn't just be legally compliant; they should reflect the heart of Christian ethics—a commitment to fairness, justice, and the equal treatment of all. These policies should explicitly define prohibited forms of discrimination, including but not limited to race, ethnicity, gender, sexual orientation, religion, age, disability, and national origin. The language used should be unambiguous, accessible, and readily understandable by all employees, regardless of their level of education or familiarity with legal terminology. Furthermore, the policies must outline clear reporting procedures, guaranteeing confidentiality and protection from retaliation for those who come forward. Beyond the written policies, the culture of the organization must actively reflect these values.

This requires consistent training and education for all employees, from the CEO to entry-level staff. Training programs should go beyond simply checking boxes; they should facilitate genuine understanding and empathy, challenging ingrained biases and promoting a culture of respect and inclusion. Role-playing scenarios, interactive discussions, and case studies can effectively demonstrate the real-world consequences of discriminatory actions and the importance of proactive intervention. These sessions should not only outline company policy but also explore the moral and ethical dimensions of discrimination through a Christian lens, emphasizing the biblical mandate to love our neighbors as ourselves. Addressing biases requires a deep self-reflection. As leaders, we must honestly assess our own potential biases—conscious or unconscious—and actively work to mitigate their influence on our decisions. This introspection is not about self-condemnation but about striving for continuous growth and improvement, acknowledging our inherent fallibility while striving to emulate Christ's example of grace and compassion. Regular self-assessments, coupled with feedback from trusted colleagues and mentors, can help identify blind spots and develop strategies for overcoming personal biases. When dealing with specific instances of discrimination or bias, a structured and compassionate approach is essential. Investigations should be thorough, impartial, and conducted with sensitivity to the individuals involved. Gathering evidence, interviewing witnesses, and meticulously documenting the process is crucial for ensuring fairness and transparency. Throughout the investigation, it's vital to maintain open communication with the individuals involved, keeping them informed of the progress and providing updates in a timely manner. The goal isn't just to determine culpability but to address the underlying issues that allowed discriminatory behavior to occur in the first place. Discipline for discriminatory actions should be consistent with the severity of the offense and in line with company policy. However, even in situations requiring disciplinary action, the Christian principle of restorative justice should guide our approach. This means prioritizing reconciliation and healing over simply punitive measures. While accountability is vital, focusing solely on punishment may not address the root causes of the behavior or promote a culture of genuine understanding and empathy.

Restorative justice seeks to repair the harm caused by the discriminatory act and to promote healing and reconciliation among those involved. This might involve mediation, facilitated discussions, or other restorative practices designed to foster understanding and promote forgiveness.

For instance, if a manager made a discriminatory remark to an employee, a restorative justice approach might involve a facilitated conversation where the manager acknowledges their wrongdoing, apologizes sincerely, and commits to changing their behavior.

The employees would also have an opportunity to share their experience and how the incident affected them. The focus is on repairing the relationship and creating a more inclusive environment. Furthermore, preventative measures are as important as reactive responses. This requires creating a culture where employees feel empowered to challenge discriminatory behavior when they witness it. Bystander intervention training can equip employees with the skills and confidence to address microaggressions and other subtle forms of discrimination before they escalate into more serious incidents. This training can provide practical strategies for intervening safely and effectively, emphasizing the importance of speaking up while also prioritizing the safety and well-being of the intervener. Beyond formal policies and training, the leadership style itself plays a critical role in preventing and addressing discrimination. Servant leadership, a cornerstone of Christian leadership, emphasizes putting the needs of others first. A servant leader actively listens to employees, values their perspectives, and creates a safe space for open communication. This approach fosters trust and mutual respect, reducing the likelihood of discriminatory behavior occurring.

IT'S ABOUT LEADING by example, demonstrating a commitment to fairness, justice, and inclusivity in every interaction and decision. Finally, remember that fostering an inclusive workplace isn't a one-time event; it's an ongoing journey. Regular reviews of policies, training programs, and leadership practices are essential to ensure that they remain relevant and effective.

Seeking external feedback from diversity and inclusion experts can provide valuable insights and identify areas for improvement.

It's an iterative process of continuous

learning, adaptation, and striving towards a more just and equitable workplace that reflects the values of our faith and the inherent dignity of every human being. Our commitment to building a workplace where every individual feels valued, respected, and empowered is a testament to our faith and a tangible expression of God's love in action. The journey toward true inclusion may be challenging, but the reward—a workplace that truly reflects the image of God—is immeasurable.

It requires sustained effort, consistent vigilance, and a steadfast commitment to living out our Christian values in every aspect of our leadership. This is not just a matter of legal compliance; it is a moral imperative rooted in our faith and a testament to the transformative power of Christian principles in the workplace.

Handling Difficult Employee Performance Issues

Addressing performance issues within a team presents

unique challenges, especially when viewed through a lens of faith. As Christian leaders, our approach should be guided not only by company policy but also by the principles of compassion, fairness, and restorative justice. This isn't about simply adhering to HR protocols; it's about treating each individual with the dignity and respect they deserve as a child of God. We strive not only to correct performance deficiencies but also to help the employee grow, both professionally and spiritually. The goal is restoration, not retribution.

Before confronting a performance issue, prayerful reflection is crucial. Seeking God's wisdom and guidance allows us to approach the situation with clarity and discernment, enabling us to identify the root causes of the problem and choose the most compassionate and effective course of action. This involves understanding the individual's circumstances, pressures, and personal struggles, remembering that we are all flawed humans navigating life's complexities. Perhaps there are underlying personal issues affecting their work –family problems, health concerns, or financial difficulties. A compassionate approach involves seeking to understand these factors before jumping to judgment. It is important to listen actively, showing empathy and a genuine desire to help.

This may involve initiating a private conversation to understand their perspective and any challenges they're facing, thus creating a safe and trusting environment for open communication. The process of addressing performance issues should be transparent and documented. While maintaining confidentiality where appropriate, transparency builds trust and prevents misunderstandings. Keeping a clear record of conversations, agreed-upon actions, and progress (or lack thereof) protects both the employee and the organization.

This documentation should be detailed yet compassionate, reflecting the effort made to support the employees' growth. It's a record of a journey of restoration, not simply a file of disciplinary actions. Remember, the goal is to help the individual improve, not to build a case against them. Fairness is paramount. Consistent application of performance standards across the team is essential to avoid accusations of bias or favoritism. If one employee receives a reprimand for a particular infraction, similar infractions from other team members should be addressed with equal firmness and consistency. However, fairness doesn't necessitate identical treatment; it necessitates equitable treatment. Individual circumstances should always be considered. A fair process ensures that employees understand the expectations and the consequences of failing to meet those expectations. This requires clear communication of performance standards and regular feedback, not just during performance reviews, but throughout the year.

Regular check-ins provide opportunities to address concerns early, preventing minor issues from escalating into major problems. Restorative justice is the ultimate goal. Instead of focusing solely on punishment, we aim for reconciliation and rehabilitation. This approach emphasizes repairing the harm caused by poor performance and restoring the employee to their full potential. This might involve providing additional training, mentoring, or opportunities for professional development. It's about investing in the employee's growth and empowering them to succeed. This isn't a passive

approach; it requires active engagement, providing resources and support to enable the employee to overcome their challenges. It's a testament to our belief in their inherent worth and potential for growth. Often, the most challenging performance issues stem from behavioral problems, rather than simply a lack of skill or competency.

These situations demand a careful, prayerful approach. Before taking any action, I take time for personal reflection and prayer, seeking God's guidance on how to respond in a manner consistent with His love and justice. This may involve seeking counsel from trusted mentors or colleagues – both within and outside of the organization – to gain different perspectives and ensure that my actions are fair and appropriate. If the behavioral issues stem from personal struggles, such as addiction or mental health challenges, it's essential to show compassion and understanding.

It might be necessary to connect the employee with resources to address these underlying problems. This could involve referring them to employee assistance programs (EAPs) or other relevant support systems. We have a responsibility to provide resources and support that could enable the employee to address their personal struggles, facilitating both their personal and professional growth. This is not just about improving workplace performance; it's about caring for the whole person, body, mind, and spirit.

If despite all efforts, the employee's performance doesn't improve, we must consider the implications. While our approach is compassionate, it must also be firm and consistent. There are times when, despite our best intentions and efforts, an employee's behavior or performance is simply incompatible with the workplace. In such cases, difficult decisions may need to be made, keeping in mind the employee's dignity and worth throughout the process. This might involve a performance improvement plan, temporary suspension, or even termination. Even in such difficult circumstances, our approach must remain rooted in faith, demonstrating empathy and care, even as we uphold organizational standards. Throughout the entire process, remember the importance of prayer and seeking God's guidance. Pray for the employee, for wisdom in your decisions, and for strength to navigate the complexities of the situation. Remember, you are not alone; God is with you, providing the strength and wisdom you need to make sound, compassionate, and ethically responsible decisions. Addressing difficult performance issues within a Christian framework necessitates an approach rooted in grace and truth. It's about upholding organizational standards while maintaining a deep respect for the inherent dignity of every individual.

It's about recognizing that both grace and truth are essential in leading with faith and integrity. Grace, in the sense of extending compassion and understanding, and truth, in the sense of adhering to standards and expectations. Sometimes, the challenge isn't a single, easily identifiable issue but a pattern of inconsistent performance or problematic behavior. Identifying underlying causes can be more complex in these instances. It may require a thorough review of performance data, a series of conversations with the employee, and possibly input from colleagues who have interacted with the individual.

HOW BEING A CHRISTIAN MADE ME A GREAT HR LEADER

The goal is to paint a complete picture of the performance, identifying trends and patterns that might otherwise be overlooked. Each situation is unique, requiring discernment and prayerful consideration. There's no one-size-fits-all solution; the appropriate response will vary depending on the specific circumstances, the employee's personality, and the organization's policies. This is where experience and wisdom are particularly valuable. Building a support network of trusted advisors – both within and outside of the organization– can provide valuable perspectives and help ensure that the decisions you make are wise and compassionate. Another critical aspect is the importance of self-reflection. After each performance issue, I engage in personal reflection, seeking to understand my role in the situation and how I could have responded differently. This practice fosters continuous improvement and prevents any unintended consequences stemming from personal biases or unchecked reactions.

It's a reminder of our own fallibility and a call to humility.

We're all flawed humans, and we must always strive to approach each situation with compassion, understanding, and a commitment to acting in accordance with Christian principles. Even seemingly minor issues can escalate into significant problems if left unchecked. It's essential to address performance concerns promptly and proactively. Regular communication, feedback, and performance evaluations create a culture of accountability and prevent minor issues from becoming major disruptions.

This proactive approach minimizes conflicts and reduces the likelihood of larger performance problems arising. It's also about fostering a culture of trust and open communication, where employees feel comfortable approaching their managers with concerns, reducing the likelihood of problems escalating unchecked. The goal is always restoration, both for the employee and for the workplace. By combining clear expectations with compassionate support, we create an environment where employees can thrive, both professionally and personally.

When we approach performance management with a faith-based perspective, it's not merely about achieving

compliance or maximizing productivity; it's about nurturing the people entrusted to our care and supporting them in their journey of growth and development. This holistic approach, rooted in Christian values, produces a workplace characterized by both excellence and compassion. The result is a more engaged, productive, and spiritually enriched environment for everyone involved. The process isn't solely about correcting mistakes, but about enabling individuals to reach their full potential and become the best versions of themselves, reflecting God's love and grace in their work and in their lives. This approach, grounded in faith, offers a powerful framework for navigating the complexities of employee performance management and cultivating a thriving, ethically sound workplace.

Maintaining Confidentiality and Protecting Employee Privacy

Maintaining confidentiality and protecting employee privacy are paramount, not merely as legal requirements but as

expressions of our Christian commitment to respecting the dignity and worth of each individual. This isn't simply about avoiding lawsuits; it's about upholding the inherent value of every person as a beloved child of God. In the HR context, this translates to a rigorous commitment to data security, ethical information handling, and fostering a culture of trust and respect. This begins with clear, transparent policies regarding data collection and usage. Employees need to understand what information is being collected, why it's being collected, how it will be used, and who will have access to it. This transparency is not just a legal necessity; it's a demonstration of our commitment to honesty and integrity. We cannot expect trust if we are not forthright about our data practices. Our approach to data security should reflect the seriousness with which we would protect any personal information entrusted to us outside the workplace. We wouldn't casually share a friend's medical information or financial details; neither should we treat employee data with less care. This requires robust security measures, including secure storage, access controls, and regular security audits. We need to be proactive, not reactive, in protecting sensitive information. This includes staying current with best practices in data security and investing in the necessary technologies and training to ensure that our systems are secure. Furthermore, we must educate our employees about their own role in maintaining data security. This includes training on password security, phishing awareness, and the importance of reporting any suspicious activity. Education is not a one-time event; it's an ongoing process requiring regular reinforcement and updates. Beyond data security, the ethical handling of employee information extends to how we use that information. We must be mindful of the potential for bias and discrimination. For instance, when making decisions about hiring, promotion, or performance evaluations, we must ensure that our decisions are based on objective criteria and not influenced by personal biases or irrelevant information. We should regularly review our processes to identify and mitigate potential biases. This requires a level of self-awareness and a willingness to examine our own perspectives. This mirrors the biblical call for self-reflection and the pursuit of righteousness. We are called to be just and impartial, avoiding any form of favoritism or prejudice. Confidentiality extends beyond data to encompass conversations and observations.

We must treat all employee information with the utmost discretion. This means avoiding gossip, refraining from sharing confidential information with unauthorized individuals, and respecting the privacy of employee conversations. In situations where we have concerns about an employee's well-being or potential misconduct, we must follow established procedures and handle sensitive information with care and sensitivity. It's crucial to remember that while we are responsible for upholding company policies and procedures, we must also adhere to our Christian values. Our aim is not to punish or condemn but to restore and help individuals to grow. This requires patience, empathy, and a deep understanding of the human condition.

The principle of "loving your neighbor" finds practical application in how we handle employee grievances and concerns. We should create an environment where employees feel safe to voice their concerns without fear of retribution. This requires establishing clear channels for communication, actively listening to employee concerns, and taking appropriate action to address them. Sometimes this involves mediating disputes, sometimes it involves referring employees to appropriate resources, and sometimes it simply involves offering a listening ear and providing support. The goal is not to simply resolve the immediate conflict but to build stronger, more trusting relationships within the team.

This is a reflection of the restorative justice approach emphasized in the Bible. Instead of focusing on punishment, we aim to repair the damage and restore harmony.

We seek to understand the underlying issues contributing to the conflict and to find solutions that are beneficial to all parties involved. This process requires patience, understanding, and a willingness to forgive. An important aspect of maintaining confidentiality and protecting employee privacy is understanding the legal framework surrounding data protection.

Legislation like GDPR and CCPA provides a clear outline of legal requirements, setting specific standards for data collection, usage, and storage. Familiarity with these regulations is crucial, not only to avoid legal repercussions but also to ensure that our practices align with ethical principles. We must understand the requirements for consent, data minimization, and data security, and implement procedures to ensure full compliance. This is not simply a matter of ticking boxes; it reflects our commitment to upholding the law and respecting the rights of our employees. Furthermore, regular updates and training on these regulations are

necessary to ensure that our processes remain current and effective. The ever-evolving landscape of data protection necessitates ongoing education and vigilance. Beyond legal requirements, we must consider the ethical implications of technology usage in the workplace. Monitoring employee activity, including email, internet usage, and communications, raises significant ethical concerns. Transparency and informed consent are vital. Employees must understand what is being monitored and why. A balance must be struck between legitimate business needs and the privacy rights of employees.

Consider implementing monitoring tools only when there's a genuine and specific need. And before implementation, conduct thorough risk assessments to evaluate the necessity and proportionality of any surveillance activities. Always follow due process and only use monitoring tools in accordance with legal and ethical standards. Consider the potential for misinterpretation and implement procedures for handling complaints and grievances. Our Christian values should guide us to favor transparency and fairness, ensuring that any monitoring measures are implemented ethically and with sensitivity. Another crucial area is the handling of sensitive employee data, such as medical information, personal financial details, and disciplinary records. Strict access controls are essential, limiting access to those who have a legitimate need to know. This information should be stored securely and handled with the utmost discretion. We must adhere to all relevant data protection regulations and ensure that all employees involved in handling sensitive data are adequately trained.

This isn't solely a matter of complying with regulations; it is a reflection of our Christian duty to protect the vulnerable and to treat all information with the respect it deserves. This also includes regular audits and reviews of our data handling procedures to ensure that our practices remain ethical and compliant. Finally, fostering a culture of trust and respect is perhaps the most critical aspect of maintaining confidentiality and protecting employee privacy. This involves creating an open and honest environment where employees feel comfortable raising concerns about data protection practices. Establish clear reporting channels for any data breaches or security concerns. This encourages a culture of accountability and transparency, promoting a workplace where employees feel valued, and their rights respected. Ultimately, our approach to data protection should reflect our Christian values, demonstrating our commitment to respecting the dignity and worth of everyone. By integrating faith and ethical business practices, we create a workplace characterized by both integrity and trust.

This extends beyond legal compliance; it signifies our genuine commitment to the well-being of our employees and the upholding of ethical principles in all our interactions. Our actions should consistently reflect our belief that every employee is a person of worth, deserving of respect and compassion.

Legal and Ethical Compliance in HR

Building upon the foundation of confidentiality and privacy, we now delve into the broader landscape of legal and ethical compliance within the HR function.

This isn't merely about navigating a minefield of regulations; it's about aligning our actions with both the letter and the spirit of the law, guided by our Christian faith. This integration isn't a matter of compartmentalizing our beliefs and our professional responsibilities; rather, it's about recognizing that our faith informs and enriches every aspect of our lives, including our work in HR. The legal framework governing HR practices is extensive and varies depending on location and industry.

However, some core principles remain consistent: fairness, transparency, and respect for individual rights. These principles align directly with our Christian values. Fairness, for instance, isn't just about equal opportunity; it's about treating everyone with the compassion and understanding that Christ teaches us. It's about recognizing that every person is unique and deserves to be valued for their individual contributions and potential. This extends beyond legal compliance to encompass creating an inclusive environment where everyone feels respected and valued.

In practice, this means actively seeking to understand and address any biases that might inadvertently influence hiring, promotion, or disciplinary actions. Regular reviews of our HR processes can help to identify and mitigate such biases, ensuring that our decisions are based on merit and not prejudice. For instance, using structured interviews and standardized evaluation methods minimizes the impact of unconscious bias. Furthermore, establishing clear and objective performance criteria ensures fairness in

performance appraisals and promotions. Training managers and HR staff on diversity, equity, and inclusion best practices further reinforces this commitment to fairness. Transparency is another cornerstone of both legal compliance and ethical HR practices. Employees have a right to understand the rules and policies that govern their employment. This is not simply a legal requirement; it's an act of respect and trust. Open communication about company policies, procedures, and expectations builds confidence and fosters a positive work environment.

Regularly reviewing and updating employee handbooks, ensuring clarity and accessibility, is crucial. Furthermore, transparent communication regarding changes in company policy or structure helps employees understand the rationale behind the changes, promoting acceptance and collaboration.

Transparency also applies to disciplinary processes and performance management. Clear and consistent communication ensures that employees understand the expectations and consequences of their actions.

THIS IS ESSENTIAL FOR fostering accountability and trust. For example, clearly defining what constitutes acceptable behavior in the workplace and outlining a fair and consistent disciplinary process avoids misunderstandings and promotes fairness. Respect for individual rights is essential. Federal and state laws, in addition to company policies, protect employees' rights to privacy, freedom from discrimination, and fair treatment. Our Christian faith reinforces this imperative, calling us to treat each person with dignity and respect.

Respecting employee privacy extends far beyond legal mandates; it is a reflection of our faith's emphasis on the inherent worth of each individual.

For example, conducting thorough background checks only, when necessary, with proper consent and transparency, respects an individual's privacy while ensuring workplace safety. Similarly, maintaining confidentiality in all employee matters is crucial; our commitment to safeguarding private information underscores our respect for the individual's dignity. Beyond these core principles, legal and ethical compliance in HR encompasses a wide range of specific areas.

Compensation and benefits must adhere to all relevant laws and regulations, ensuring fair and equitable pay practices.

This includes transparency in compensation structures, adherence to minimum wage laws, and compliance with regulations concerning overtime pay and benefits. Regular audits of compensation practices can help identify and correct any discrepancies or inequities.

Similarly, health and safety regulations must be strictly adhered to, providing employees with a safe and healthy work environment.

This includes implementing safety protocols, providing appropriate training, and proactively addressing any safety concerns raised by employees. Employment practices, such as hiring, promotion, and termination, must be conducted in a fair and equitable manner, free from discrimination or retaliation. This requires adherence to equal opportunity laws, affirmative action policies

(where applicable), and careful attention to avoid biased decision-making. Consistent and documented evaluation processes, transparent interview protocols, and objective performance reviews are critical in mitigating potential biases. In addition, strong anti-harassment and anti-discrimination policies are essential, ensuring a workplace free from intimidation and offensive behavior. These policies should be clearly communicated, regularly reviewed, and vigorously enforced. Regular training programs on harassment prevention and respectful workplace behavior further reinforce this commitment to a safe and inclusive workplace. Managing employee relationships requires careful attention to legal and ethical considerations. Confidential and objective disciplinary procedures are essential, ensuring fair and equitable treatment of all employees. Consistent application of company policies and procedures is paramount, along with a commitment to due process and transparency. Effective communication and a collaborative approach in resolving workplace disputes can mitigate potential legal issues and foster a more positive and harmonious work environment. Providing avenues for conflict resolution, such as mediation or arbitration, can be beneficial in facilitating resolution while respecting the rights of all parties involved. Finally, legal and ethical compliance isn't a static process; it requires ongoing vigilance and adaptation. Staying abreast of changing laws and regulations, proactively updating company policies, and providing regular training to HR staff and managers are crucial for maintaining compliance.

Regular audits of HR practices can help to identify areas for improvement and prevent potential legal issues. Investing in HR technology can streamline processes, enhance data security, and improve compliance. Furthermore, seeking advice from legal counsel, when necessary, ensures that all HR practices are compliant with relevant laws and regulations. This proactive approach to compliance demonstrates a commitment not only to meeting legal requirements but also to upholding ethical principles and fostering a culture of trust and integrity within the organization. This commitment to excellence in HR management reflects the highest ideals of Christian leadership—serving others with compassion, integrity, and unwavering commitment to justice and fairness.

By integrating our faith with our professional responsibilities, we create a workplace that reflects the values we hold dear, providing a supportive and productive environment for all employees.

HOW BEING A CHRISTIAN MADE ME A GREAT HR LEADER

Maintaining Company Culture During Growth

The transition from a company of 500 employees to one boasting 2500 presents a unique set of challenges. Growth, while exhilarating, can easily dilute the carefully cultivated culture that has been the bedrock of your success. This isn't just about maintaining the status quo; it's about proactively shaping a culture that can thrive amidst expansion. My experience in navigating this transition, guided by my faith, has taught me the importance of intentional strategies to preserve—and even enhance—our core values as our team grew. The key is not just scaling operations but scaling *values*.

One of the first challenges we faced was the dilution of communication. In a smaller company, informal

communication flowed naturally. Everyone knew what was happening, and a sense of camaraderie was easily fostered. But as the company expanded, this organic communication started to break down. We needed a more structured approach, yet one that didn't sacrifice the feeling of connection and community. We implemented several key strategies to counteract this.

Firstly, we invested heavily in technology to improve communication. This wasn't just about adopting new software; it was about choosing tools that fostered

interaction and transparency. We moved away from email-heavy communication and embraced platforms that encouraged real-time collaboration and open dialogue. Internal forums and dedicated channels for different teams facilitated better knowledge sharing and provided spaces for employees to interact and build relationships, even across different departments. This helped bridge the communication gap between the initial 500 employees and the newly joined 2000. Secondly, we didn't just rely on technology. We understood the importance of face-to-face interaction. We organized regular company-wide meetings, smaller team-building activities, and informal social gatherings. These events weren't just fun; they were strategically designed to foster a sense of community and belonging. We consciously created opportunities for employees from different teams and departments to interact, building relationships and strengthening connections. Beyond our day-to-day operations, we recognized a critical need to transform our company's cultural foundation. What had previously existed as an unspoken understanding needed deliberate definition and clarity. We crafted our company values with intention, creating more than just a static list of aspirational statements. Instead, we developed a dynamic, living document that illuminated how our core principles came to life through actual workplace experiences. This wasn't a perfunctory exercise in corporate messaging, but a meaningful exploration of what truly defined our organizational identity. The values document became far more than digital wall decor. We integrated it strategically into our most critical people processes—embedding it deeply into our onboarding experience, professional development programs, and performance evaluation framework. By weaving these principles into the fabric of our organizational culture, we ensured they weren't just words, but a genuine operational compass. What made our approach unique was our commitment to storytelling. We didn't just state values; we illustrated them through real, concrete examples of employees who had authentically embodied these principles. These narratives did more than explain—they inspired. They provided tangible guidance for longtime team members and created a clear cultural roadmap for new colleagues. This deliberate approach transformed our values from abstract concepts into a practical, meaningful guide for how we work, interact, and grow together. One crucial aspect of maintaining our culture during growth was onboarding. As we expanded, the onboarding process needed to be highly effective. We didn't just want to get new employees up to speed in their jobs; we wanted them to embrace our culture and feel like integral members of the team. Our onboarding program incorporated elements of our company's history, mission, and values. It also included opportunities for new employees to connect with established team members through mentorship programs. This approach helped ensure that everyone, regardless of their start date, understood and embraced our shared values. Another crucial element was recognizing and rewarding those who exemplified our values. We instituted an internal recognition program that celebrated employees who consistently demonstrated the characteristics we valued most. This wasn't simply about financial rewards; we also recognized individuals through public acknowledgment, feature stories in our internal newsletter, and opportunities for professional development.

By visibly celebrating these behaviors, we reinforced the importance of our values within the broader culture. A significant part of my leadership philosophy, deeply

rooted in my faith, involves servant leadership. As our

organization grew, ensuring this leadership style scaled effectively was critical. We fostered a culture of

empowerment, delegating responsibilities and providing employees with the autonomy to make decisions within their roles. This not only increased efficiency but also fostered ownership and engagement. We provided training and development opportunities that enabled our employees to grow professionally and contribute meaningfully to the organization's success. This empowerment empowered our people and ensured that our values were not merely top-down dictates but organically embraced throughout the organization.

Transparency is also essential when a company is expanding. Keeping employees informed about the company's progress, challenges, and future plans is crucial for maintaining trust and engagement. We implemented regular updates from leadership, town hall meetings, and open forums for feedback and questions. This consistent communication helped keep everyone informed and engaged, particularly important as our growth increased the complexity of the organization. It counteracted any potential for rumors or speculation and fostered a stronger sense of unity. Managing growth also necessitated adapting our leadership style. In a smaller company, a more hands-on approach was effective. But as the company grew, I recognized the need to transition to a more decentralized leadership model. This involved empowering mid-level managers and providing them with the resources and support they needed to lead their teams effectively. This was a conscious effort to delegate authority while simultaneously ensuring the integrity of our values across various departments. We offered extensive leadership training focused not just on managerial skills, but also on integrating our core values into their leadership styles. This process wasn't without its challenges. Maintaining a strong company culture during rapid growth requires

constant vigilance and adaptation. There were times when we stumbled, when we had to course-correct, when we learned from our mistakes. However, by continuously

revisiting our core values, investing in communication, empowering our employees, and fostering a culture of

transparency and trust, we successfully scaled our company while preserving the integrity of our shared culture. Through prayer and reflection, I sought guidance, recognizing that leading with faith provided not just moral direction but also practical wisdom to navigate complex organizational challenges. Our consistent focus on our values proved not just a moral imperative, but a strategic advantage in creating a thriving, ethical, and successful organization. This experience reaffirmed my belief that a faith-based approach to leadership is not only possible but highly effective in achieving both spiritual and professional fulfillment.

Delegation and Empowerment within a Faith Based Framework

The rapid expansion from 500 to 2500 employees

necessitated a fundamental shift in my leadership style. Micromanagement, which had been feasible with a smaller team, was now not only impractical but actively detrimental to growth.

This realization forced me to confront the crucial aspect of delegation and empowerment, a process profoundly shaped by my Christian faith. My approach wasn't merely about distributing tasks; it was about entrusting responsibilities, fostering growth, and reflecting the stewardship principles inherent in my beliefs. Delegation, within a faith-based framework, isn't about shedding burdens; it's about sharing them in a way that honors God-given talents and promotes the flourishing of each individual.

This meant carefully assessing the strengths and weaknesses of my team members, praying for discernment in matching tasks with abilities. It wasn't simply about efficiency; it was about recognizing the inherent dignity and potential in every person, mirroring God's creation. This approach required trust, a trust rooted in my faith and reinforced by observing the integrity and commitment of those I worked with. I learned to view delegation not as relinquishing control, but as an act of faith in both my team and God's plan for our organization.

Empowerment followed naturally from this perspective.

Instead of dictating solutions, I began to encourage

collaborative problem-solving, mirroring the collaborative nature of the Trinity. Team members were given the autonomy to make decisions within their areas of expertise, fostering a sense of ownership and responsibility. This wasn't about abdicating leadership; rather, it was about creating a culture of shared leadership, where everyone felt valued and empowered to contribute their unique gifts. This approach reduced the potential for burnout, a common consequence of overwhelming responsibilities. By sharing the load, I not only improved efficiency but also strengthened the overall well-being of the team. This process, however, demanded intentional strategies and open communication. Clear expectations, coupled with regular feedback and support, were paramount. I made it a point to have individual check-in meetings, creating a safe space for employees to share their challenges and celebrate their successes.

These weren't simply performance reviews; they were opportunities to mentor, provide encouragement, and offer prayer when needed. My faith provided the foundation for a genuine interest in the well-being of my team members, both professionally and personally. The lines between work life and personal life naturally blurred, as we shared joys and sorrows, creating a deeper sense of community. Transparency was another crucial component. I ensured that decisions were explained clearly, even if they weren't popular.

This fostered trust and understanding, which were essential for maintaining morale during periods of rapid change and expansion. We built a culture of open communication, encouraging feedback from all levels of the organization. This two-way communication wasn't just a management technique; it was a reflection of my belief in the value of every voice, mirroring the communal nature of the church. This inclusivity and openness-built trust allowed for the emergence of innovative ideas and solutions from within the team. Conflict resolution, an inevitable aspect of any growing organization, was handled with a similar approach. Disagreements, when addressed with empathy and patience, became opportunities for growth and reconciliation, reflecting the forgiving nature of Christian faith. We implemented conflict-resolution training that emphasized listening, understanding different perspectives, and finding common ground. Mediation efforts were always rooted in a desire for restoration and healing, mirroring the restorative justice found in scripture. These weren't just conflict-resolution strategies; they were expressions of a compassionate leadership style, grounded in the principles of forgiveness and reconciliation. Training and development played a vital role in empowering employees.

We invested in robust training programs designed to equip our team members with the skills and knowledge they needed to succeed in their roles. This wasn't just about improving productivity; it was about investing in individuals, reflecting the investment God makes in each of us. Mentorship programs, pairing experienced employees with those newer to the organization, nurtured a culture of learning and support. This created opportunities for both personal and professional growth, fostering a strong sense of community within the team.

Accountability was another key element. While empowerment allowed for autonomy, it was coupled with clear expectations and performance metrics. Regular performance reviews, conducted with sensitivity and grace, allowed for constructive feedback and identification of areas for improvement. This wasn't about judgment; it was about providing support and guidance to help each person reach their full potential. The focus was on growth and development, not just on meeting performance targets. Measuring success wasn't solely based on financial metrics.

We also tracked employee satisfaction, retention rates, and the overall health of the company culture. These qualitative measures were vital in assessing the effectiveness of our delegation and empowerment strategies. The goal wasn't simply to maximize profits but to create a thriving workplace where people felt valued, respected, and empowered to contribute their best work. The success of our company was intertwined with the well-being of our team members, reflecting our commitment to holistic growth and development.

As the company continued to grow, I refined my approach to delegation and empowerment, continually seeking guidance through prayer and reflection. I learned that the most effective leaders are those who serve their team, empowering them to grow and achieve their potential. This approach resonated deeply with my faith, which emphasizes servant leadership as a model for all followers of Christ. The principles of empathy, compassion, and forgiveness became integral to my leadership style, fostering a work environment that reflected the values I held dear.

My faith wasn't a separate aspect of my life; it was the foundation upon which my leadership style was built. The results demonstrated the power of aligning professional practice with deep-seated values. My Christian faith provided not only a moral compass but also a framework for practical leadership strategies. It influenced every aspect of my approach, from how I communicated with my team to how I resolved conflicts. By applying these principles, I witnessed firsthand how a faith-based approach to leadership can positively impact a team's productivity, morale, and overall success. The principles of servant leadership, empathy, and community fostered a work environment that was both productive and spiritually fulfilling. The expansion wasn't just about numbers; it was about cultivating a culture of faith, integrity, and shared purpose – a testament to the power of integrating faith and leadership. This approach wasn't merely a personal preference; it proved to be a highly effective strategy for building a thriving and successful organization. The synergy between faith and leadership became clear: a faith-infused approach wasn't just ethically sound; it was strategically advantageous. The success of our company was not just a testament to effective management practices, but a reflection of the positive impact that faith can have on all aspects of business leadership. The journey of scaling our company from 500 to 2500 employees taught me the profound interconnectedness of faith and leadership, proving that a principled approach not only brings spiritual fulfillment but also contributes to tangible, measurable success. It's a lesson I continue to carry forward, always striving to lead with faith, integrity, and compassion.

Building Trust and Transparency in a Larger Organization

The transition from a company of 500 employees to one boasting 2500 demanded more than just strategic planning; it demanded a radical shift in how we fostered communication and built trust.

HOW BEING A CHRISTIAN MADE ME A GREAT HR LEADER

Transparency, once a relatively straightforward process within smaller teams, has now become a complex, multi-layered challenge. Maintaining open communication channels across departments, locations, and hierarchical levels required a deliberate, strategic approach rooted in both practical HR strategies and the core values of my faith. One of the first hurdles we tackled was the implementation of a robust, multi-faceted communication strategy. Simply relying on email blasts or infrequent company-wide meetings was no longer sufficient. We needed channels that fostered two-way communication, allowing employees at all levels to share their concerns, ideas, and feedback. This wasn't just about information dissemination; it was about creating a culture of active listening and genuine engagement. Inspired by the biblical principle of community, we launched regular "town hall" meetings, both in person and via live streaming for remote employees. These weren't just top-down presentations; we structured them to encourage questions and open dialogues.

We established dedicated "Ask Me Anything" sessions with senior leadership, providing a safe space for employees to voice concerns, no matter how minor they seemed. The consistent theme running through these initiatives was vulnerability – a willingness to be transparent about both successes and failures. This approach, often viewed as risky in the business world, was grounded in my belief that authentic vulnerability builds trust. It was a reflection of the transparency and honesty that Jesus modeled in His ministry. Beyond formal channels, we focused on fostering a culture of informal communication. We encouraged cross-departmental collaboration through team-building events, casual lunches, and informal mentorship programs.

These events weren't just about socializing; they were designed to facilitate natural conversation and relationship-building, breaking down the hierarchical barriers that often stifle open communication in larger organizations. We consciously worked to build a sense of community, mirroring the fellowship found within the Christian church, where individuals from diverse backgrounds feel comfortable connecting and supporting one another.

Another critical element of building trust and transparency was ensuring consistent and equitable access to information.

In a larger organization, the risk of information silos is significant, leading to confusion, miscommunication, and ultimately, a breakdown of trust. We combatted this by implementing a comprehensive intranet system, which served as a central repository for company news, policies, procedures, and performance data. We ensured that information was accessible to all employees, regardless of their position or location.

This commitment to equal access to information wasn't just a matter of fairness; it reflected the biblical principle of justice and equity.

Transparency, however, isn't solely about information dissemination; it's also about accountability. We implemented a system of regular performance reviews, providing employees with constructive feedback and opportunities for professional growth. These reviews were not punitive; instead, they were designed to foster a culture of ongoing learning and development.

This approach was guided by my understanding of restorative justice, a concept that emphasizes rehabilitation and reconciliation over punishment. We recognized that mistakes are inevitable but addressing them constructively and transparently builds trust and strengthens the team. The emphasis was on growth, not judgment, a reflection of God's grace and mercy. Beyond performance reviews, we established clear channels for addressing grievances and conflicts.

We implemented a formal process for handling complaints, ensuring that all concerns were investigated thoroughly and impartially. This system was designed to be fair and just, reflecting the principles of biblical justice. We also invested heavily in conflict resolution training, equipping managers and employees with the skills to address disagreements constructively and respectfully. The goal wasn't merely to resolve conflicts but to prevent them from escalating and damaging relationships.

The process emphasized restoration and reconciliation, mirroring the principles of forgiveness and reconciliation found in the teachings of Christ. Furthermore, recognizing that trust is built through action, not just words, we prioritized leading by example. We consistently demonstrated transparency in our own decision-making processes, explaining the rationale behind our choices and welcoming feedback. We shared both our successes and our failures, acknowledging mistakes openly and learning from them collectively. This demonstrated vulnerability fostered trust and encouraged employees to be more open and honest in their own interactions. It exemplified the vulnerability Jesus demonstrated throughout His ministry, a vulnerability that built trust and fostered deep relationships with His followers. The process of building trust and transparency in a larger organization is an ongoing journey, not a destination.

It requires consistent effort, ongoing commitment, and a willingness to adapt and improve. But the rewards are immeasurable. A culture of trust and transparency fosters a more engaged, productive, and loyal workforce. It improves morale, reduces conflict, and enhances creativity and innovation. Moreover, this approach aligns perfectly with my Christian faith, reflecting the values of integrity, honesty, and community that I strive to live by.

In my experience, the most impactful actions often stem from seemingly small gestures. For instance, we established an anonymous feedback mechanism where employees could share their thoughts and concerns without fear of retribution.

This initiative, while seemingly minor, demonstrated our genuine commitment to listening and responding to the concerns of our employees.

This act of providing a safe space for feedback is a direct reflection of the parable of the lost sheep, emphasizing the value of each individual within the larger community. Furthermore, we actively sought feedback on our

communication strategies themselves. We conducted regular surveys and focus groups to assess the effectiveness of our efforts and identify areas for improvement. This demonstrated a commitment to continuous improvement, ensuring that our communication practices remained relevant and effective in meeting the evolving needs of our diverse workforce.

This continuous refinement mirrors the ongoing process of spiritual growth and refinement, which is a core tenant of Christian faith. The growth of our organization from 500 to 2500 employees was not simply a matter of increasing headcount; it was a journey of building and nurturing a strong, cohesive community. The challenges of maintaining trust and transparency in this expanded context were significant, but by integrating my faith-based principles of community, empathy, and accountability into our HR strategies, we were able to build a more connected and engaged workforce. The result was not simply a larger organization; it was a thriving community rooted in mutual respect, trust, and shared purpose. The principles of servant leadership, guided by my faith, played a central role in navigating this transformative period, demonstrating that a faith-infused approach to leadership isn't just ethically sound; it's strategically advantageous, yielding a more engaged and productive workforce.

THE SUCCESS WE EXPERIENCED was a direct testament to the power of integrating faith and leadership, fostering a work environment where both professional success and spiritual growth could flourish simultaneously. This journey underscores the profound interconnectedness of faith and leadership, showing that a principled approach not only brings spiritual fulfillment but also leads to tangible, measurable success within the organization.

Adapting Leadership Styles to Different Team Sizes and Dynamics

The exponential growth from 500 to 2500 employees wasn't simply a matter of adding bodies; it was a fundamental shift in organizational dynamics. The intimate, almost familial atmosphere of the smaller company began to fragment as new departments, teams, and hierarchical levels emerged.

MY LEADERSHIP STYLE, effective in a smaller setting where direct interaction and personal connection were readily available, needed a significant recalibration.

What worked when I could know each employee personally, understand their individual struggles and aspirations, and directly address concerns, proved less effective in navigating the complexities of a much larger, more geographically dispersed workforce. This necessitated a transition from a highly individualized, hands-on approach to a more strategic, systems-oriented leadership style. The challenge wasn't to abandon the personal touch entirely, but to adapt it to a scale that prioritized efficiency and consistency while retaining the essential elements of empathy and care that had defined our previous success. This adaptation involved embracing delegation on a much larger scale. In the smaller company, I often found myself personally handling many tasks, from conflict resolution to performance reviews. This level of personal involvement was no longer feasible.

Therefore, I focused on building strong leadership teams within each department. My role shifted from directly managing individual employees to empowering and equipping departmental leaders.

This required careful selection of individuals who not only possessed the technical skills but also demonstrated the character traits – integrity, compassion, and a servant's heart– that aligned with our organizational values. My faith played a pivotal role in this selection process, guiding me towards individuals who demonstrated a commitment to ethical conduct and a genuine care for the well-being of their team members. It was about identifying individuals who reflected the Christian principles of stewardship and responsibility, entrusting them with the well-being of their respective teams. Training and development became paramount. Equipping these leaders with the necessary tools and skills to manage their teams effectively was crucial. This included not only managerial training but also coaching on conflict resolution, performance management, and fostering a positive team culture. We implemented a robust training program incorporating both technical skills development and leadership workshops focusing on emotional intelligence, communication, and ethical decision-making. This program was designed to create a unified leadership approach across the organization, ensuring consistency in how teams were managed, and employees were supported. Moreover, integrating our Christian values into the training emphasized the importance of ethical leadership, promoting a culture of fairness, respect, and accountability. We used biblical principles of servant leadership, emphasizing the importance of putting the needs of others first and leading by example.

Communication strategies also required a complete overhaul. The informal, casual communication channels that worked effectively in the smaller company were inadequate for a workforce of 2500. We implemented a multi-pronged approach, incorporating regular company-wide emails, departmental meetings, and quarterly town halls.

These communication channels were used not merely to disseminate information but also to create opportunities for two-way dialogue. Feedback mechanisms were established to ensure that employee voices were heard and concerns addressed promptly. Regular surveys, suggestion boxes, and open forums were created to encourage open communication and transparency. The aim was to build a culture where employees felt safe and empowered to express their ideas and concerns without fear of retribution. This was fundamentally rooted in our shared faith, creating a sense of community and belonging, even across the larger and more complex organizational structure. Building and maintaining trust in this expanded environment demanded a proactive and transparent approach.

Regular updates on company performance, strategic initiatives, and challenges were shared across all levels of the organization. Openness and honesty were paramount, fostering a sense of shared responsibility and accountability. This transparency wasn't just a matter of compliance; it reflected our commitment to operating with integrity, a core value rooted in our faith. We established clear communication protocols, ensuring that important information was disseminated quickly and accurately, while also creating a safe space for feedback and constructive criticism. This emphasis on open communication and trust extended beyond simply sharing information; it involved actively listening to employee concerns and responding with empathy and understanding. Conflict resolution, once managed largely on a case-by-case basis, became a more formal and structured process. We established clear procedures for handling grievances and disputes, ensuring that all employees had access to fair and impartial processes. Mediation and conflict resolution training were implemented for both managers and employees, empowering them to navigate conflicts constructively and compassionately. The emphasis was always on restoring relationships, not simply resolving the immediate issue. This mirrored our faith-based approach to conflict resolution, which prioritizes reconciliation and forgiveness. We strived to create an environment where disagreements could be addressed in a respectful manner, promoting understanding and empathy between conflicting parties. The shift in leadership style also required a conscious effort to prioritize my own well-being. The demands of leading a larger organization were significantly greater, and I realized the importance of establishing clear boundaries to prevent burnout. This involved delegating effectively, prioritizing tasks, and making time for personal reflection and rejuvenation. My faith played a crucial role in this process, providing me with the strength and resilience to navigate the challenges of leadership while maintaining my own spiritual and emotional health. Regular prayer, meditation, and time spent with my family were essential in preventing burnout and maintaining a balanced lifestyle. I recognized that true leadership involved not only serving others but also caring for oneself. Moreover, the growth necessitated a deeper consideration of succession planning. We needed to cultivate and develop future leaders within the organization to ensure long-term sustainability. This involved identifying high-potential employees and providing them with opportunities for growth and development. Mentorship programs and leadership training were established to equip these individuals with the necessary skills and experience to assume leadership roles in the future. This commitment to succession planning not only ensured the continuity of the organization but also fostered a culture of ongoing learning and development. It was essential to identify individuals who not only possessed the technical skills but also embodied our organizational values, ensuring that our Christian principles would continue to guide the organization's future leadership. Scaling our organization while maintaining our core values wasn't simply about adapting to a larger size; it was about adapting our leadership approach to effectively guide, support, and inspire a significantly larger workforce. This transition required a strategic shift, moving from a more hands-on, individualized approach to a more systems-oriented style that prioritized delegation, training, communication, and fostering a strong leadership pipeline. However, throughout this transformation, my faith remained a constant guide, shaping my decision-making, informing my leadership style, and influencing the values that permeated our organizational culture. The integration of faith and leadership proved not only ethically sound but also strategically advantageous, creating a thriving work environment where both professional success and spiritual growth could flourish. The result was not just a larger company; it was a stronger, more resilient, and ultimately more successful organization, built on a foundation of faith, trust, and shared purpose. The journey demonstrated the transformative power of integrating faith-based principles into every aspect of leadership, proving that a principled approach not only brings spiritual fulfillment but also tangible, measurable success.

This was a testament to the interconnectedness of faith and leadership, showing that a truly successful leader prioritizes both the spiritual and professional well-being of their team, creating an environment where both can flourish.

SCALING WITH INTEGRITY and Faith

The transition from a company of 500 to one encompassing 2500 employees was not merely an increase in headcount; it was a metamorphosis. The close-knit, almost familial atmosphere of our smaller organization, where I knew each employee personally, began to dissipate as the company grew. This expansion necessitated a shift from my highly individualized, hands-on leadership style to a more strategic, system-oriented approach. The challenge wasn't to abandon the personal connection entirely, but to adapt it to a scale that prioritized both efficiency and the empathetic, caring culture we had cultivated. This wasn't a simple matter of implementing new management software or restructuring departments. It was a profound change that demanded a re-evaluation of our core values and how they manifested themselves in our daily operations. My faith, a constant throughout my career, guided this transition.

I drew strength from scriptures like **Proverbs 16:3**, *"Commit to the Lord whatever you do, and he will establish your plans."* This wasn't just a personal mantra; it became a guiding principle for our entire HR team. One of the most significant changes involved our hiring practices. With rapid growth, we needed to streamline the recruitment process while maintaining our commitment to hiring individuals who aligned with our company values, both professionally and ethically. We implemented a more rigorous, multi-stage interview process, incorporating assessments to evaluate not only skills and experience but also cultural fit and character. This was crucial in maintaining the integrity of our team and ensuring that our new hires shared our commitment to excellence and ethical conduct. We found ourselves increasingly relying on behavioral interview questions, probing for examples of how candidates had demonstrated honesty, integrity, and compassion in previous roles. This approach went beyond simply assessing technical skills; it was about identifying individuals who embodied the principles we held dear. Furthermore, we established mentorship programs to foster a culture of support and guidance within our expanding workforce. Senior employees were paired with newer hires, offering invaluable support and guidance, fostering a sense of community and shared purpose. This initiative was particularly important as our company grew geographically, creating a greater need for connection and collaboration across different locations.

We incorporated regular team-building activities designed to foster camaraderie and strengthen relationships amongst colleagues. These events weren't merely social gatherings; they were strategic opportunities to reinforce our shared values and build a stronger, more cohesive team. We found that investing time in these initiatives was not only valuable in terms of employee morale and retention but also contributed to improved productivity and teamwork. This was a direct application of biblical principles of community and mutual support, fostering a workplace that felt less like a corporate machine and more like a collaborative effort among colleagues striving toward a common goal. Another key element of this scaling process was the development of clear communication channels. As the company grew, the risk of miscommunication and

information silos increased. To mitigate this, we invested heavily in improving our internal communication systems. We implemented regular company-wide updates, transparently sharing information about the company's performance, challenges, and future plans. We also created opportunities for open dialogue and feedback from employees through regular surveys, suggestion boxes, and town hall meetings. This demonstrated our commitment to inclusivity and open communication, making employees feel valued and heard. Transparency and open communication were integral to maintaining trust and ensuring that our employees felt they were part of a larger purpose. This directly mirrored the biblical emphasis on truthfulness and open communication.

Our commitment to ethical conduct and integrity extended to our approach to compensation and benefits. We aimed to create a compensation structure that was not only competitive but also equitable and fair. We regularly reviewed our salaries and benefits packages to ensure they aligned with industry standards and reflected our commitment to valuing our employees. We sought to treat our employees with respect and dignity, recognizing their value as individuals and not just cogs in a machine. We believed that fair compensation wasn't just a matter of legal compliance; it was a reflection of our Christian values of justice and equity. This emphasis on fair treatment fostered loyalty and reduced employee turnover, a significant factor in managing a rapidly expanding workforce. Dealing with conflict was another area where our values played a crucial role. The growth of the company inevitably led to increased interpersonal and inter-departmental conflicts. We established clear conflict resolution processes, emphasizing empathy, understanding, and restorative justice.

Our approach wasn't about assigning blame; rather, it was about fostering reconciliation and facilitating constructive dialogue to find mutually acceptable solutions. This reflected our belief in forgiveness and reconciliation, core tenets of the Christian faith. We provided training to managers on effective conflict resolution techniques, empowering them to address conflicts promptly and fairly, minimizing their impact on morale and productivity. We found that a focus on restorative justice not only resolved conflicts but also

strengthened relationships and fostered a more positive work environment. Delegation became a critical skill as our company expanded.

Recognizing my limitations as a single leader, I actively cultivated a strong leadership pipeline. This involved identifying, training, and empowering talented individuals within the organization to assume leadership roles. I focused on developing their skills, providing them with the resources and support they needed to succeed, and trusting them to make decisions. This empowerment fostered a culture of ownership and accountability, freeing me to focus on strategic initiatives and ensuring the long-term success of the company. This approach mirrored the biblical principle of discipleship and leadership development, focusing on nurturing others to reach their full potential. It wasn't about accumulating power but about distributing it responsibly, fostering a sense of shared leadership and collective responsibility. The growth of our company wasn't simply a numerical achievement; it was a testament to the transformative power of integrating faith into the workplace.

By upholding our Christian values of integrity, empathy, and servant leadership, we were able to scale our organization while maintaining a positive and productive work environment. This journey demonstrated that a principled approach to business not only enhances ethical conduct but also delivers tangible, measurable results.

Our success wasn't solely due to shrewd business strategies; it reflected the enduring power of faith and its ability to guide and inspire us in building a thriving and purposeful organization. It was a journey of faith, growth, and transformation, proving that integrating faith-based principles into leadership isn't merely a pious ideal but a powerful catalyst for building successful and impactful organizations. It's a testament that success in business and spiritual growth can indeed coexist, reinforcing a belief that one doesn't negate the other but strengthens the whole.

The journey also revealed the importance of adapting leadership styles, recognizing that what worked in a smaller company needed significant adjustments as we scaled up. The transition required a

commitment to constant learning, adaptation, and a willingness to embrace new challenges with faith as the guiding principle. Ultimately, our scaling journey wasn't just about growing the company; it was about growing in faith, wisdom, and compassion, a growth reflected in the lives of our employees and the enduring strength of our organization.

The result? Not just a larger company, but a stronger, more resilient, and ultimately, more successful one, built on a foundation of faith, trust, and shared purpose.

Mentoring and Coaching Future HR Leaders

Mentoring and coaching are not merely tasks on an HR professional's to-do list; they are vital investments in the future of any organization, and particularly so when viewed through the lens of faith. As a Christian leader, I've found that mentoring and coaching extend beyond imparting technical skills; it's about nurturing the whole person – their spiritual, emotional, and professional growth. This holistic approach, rooted in my faith, has proven

profoundly effective in shaping future HR leaders who are not only competent but also compassionate, ethical, and purpose driven. My approach to mentoring and coaching begins with prayer. Before engaging with a mentee, I dedicate time to seek God's guidance, asking for discernment to understand their needs, strengths, and challenges. This prayerful preparation helps me approach each mentoring session with empathy and a genuine desire to serve. It allows me to see beyond the immediate professional goals and perceive the deeper spiritual needs that might be influencing their performance and aspirations. For example, I once mentored a young HR professional struggling with burnout. While her initial concerns were about workload and deadlines, through prayerful reflection and conversation, we discovered that her deep-seated insecurity was contributing to her stress.

Addressing this underlying spiritual issue proved crucial to helping her regain her equilibrium and develop healthier coping mechanisms.

This involved open conversations about faith, reliance on God, and techniques for stress management rooted in spiritual practices. The core principles I emphasize during mentoring sessions are directly derived from my faith. Integrity, servant leadership, empathy, and forgiveness are not just buzzwords; they are the cornerstones of my mentoring philosophy. I share personal anecdotes, illustrating how these principles have guided me through various professional challenges. For instance, I describe instances where I had to make difficult decisions, facing ethical dilemmas, and how prayer and a reliance on biblical wisdom helped me navigate those situations with integrity. This transparency and vulnerability help build trust and create a safe space for mentees to share their own struggles. Mentoring is not a one-way street. It's a reciprocal relationship where both mentor and mentee learn and grow. I encourage my mentees to share their perspectives, challenge my assumptions, and hold me accountable. This open dialogue fosters mutual respect and strengthens the mentoring bond. I find that listening attentively is just as important as offering advice.

Sometimes, the most effective mentoring involves simply being present, offering a listening ear, and providing emotional support. It's about walking alongside them, sharing in their joys and challenges, offering a shoulder to lean on when needed. My coaching approach is similarly faith informed. I believe that every individual possesses unique talents and gifts bestowed by God.

My role as a coach is to help them discover and develop these gifts. This involves identifying their strengths and weaknesses, setting clear goals, and creating a plan to achieve those goals.

I incorporate practical tools and techniques from both the secular and faith-based world, drawing upon my experience to tailor coaching

strategies to the individual needs of each mentee. This might include goal-setting exercises, conflict resolution workshops, or simply encouraging them to engage in reflective prayer before critical decisions.

Practical applications of coaching in an HR context are numerous. I've coached several individuals on improving their communication skills, particularly during difficult conversations with employees.

We worked on role-playing scenarios, providing constructive feedback, and incorporating empathy and active listening techniques. In another instance, I coached a mentee on developing stronger leadership skills. This involved identifying their leadership style, understanding their strengths and weaknesses, and

developing a plan for improvement, which included reading relevant leadership books and attending workshops. The coaching process always incorporates a focus on ethical leadership and the application of Christian values in their decision-making processes. The mentoring and coaching process is often intertwined with spiritual development. I do not force my faith onto my mentees, but I create an environment where faith can be explored and discussed if they desire.

I share my own spiritual journey, highlighting how my faith has shaped my leadership style and helped me overcome obstacles. I encourage them to reflect on their own values and beliefs and how these influence their professional life.

This creates a space for deeper discussions about purpose, meaning, and vocation—essential elements for genuine leadership. Furthermore, the process of mentoring and coaching involves regular check-ins and feedback. I maintain open communication with my mentees, providing regular support and guidance.

We establish clear expectations and goals, and I provide constructive feedback to help them track their progress and make necessary adjustments. This ongoing support ensures that they are not only meeting their professional goals but also growing spiritually and personally. This sustained mentorship empowers them to face future challenges with resilience and confidence, drawing on the foundational principles we've explored together. The long-term impact of faith-based mentoring and coaching is profound.

IT'S ABOUT SHAPING leaders who are not only technically proficient but also ethically grounded, spiritually fulfilled, and committed to making a positive impact on the world. These leaders become beacons of integrity and compassion in their organizations, influencing their colleagues and contributing to a more just and equitable workplace. I have seen firsthand the transformative power of this approach, witnessing mentees blossom into confident, competent, and compassionate leaders who embody the values we discussed.

Their success is a testament to the power of faith-integrated leadership development. By incorporating faith into the mentoring and coaching process, we cultivate a new generation of HR leaders who are well-equipped to navigate the complexities of the modern workplace with integrity, compassion, and a deep sense of purpose. This holistic approach to leadership development ensures that future HR leaders are not only successful in their careers but also live lives of purpose and meaning.

This creates a ripple effect of positive impact throughout their organizations and beyond.

Becoming a Role Model for Ethical and Faith Based Leadership

The previous chapter explored the transformative power of faith-integrated mentoring and coaching. But true leadership isn't just about guiding others; it's about embodying the very principles you espouse.

IT'S ABOUT BECOMING a living testament to the value's you champion, allowing your actions to speak louder than words. As a Christian HR leader, this has been paramount to my success. It's not enough to simply talk about integrity, empathy, and servant leadership; I must demonstrate these qualities in every interaction, every decision, and every aspect of my work. This principle, rooted in my faith, has profoundly shaped my leadership style and profoundly impacted the teams I've led.

IT'S ABOUT CREATING a culture where ethical behavior isn't just expected, but actively modeled and celebrated. This concept of embodying ethical and faith-based leadership isn't merely theoretical; it's deeply practical. It translates into tangible actions and visible results. For instance, during a period of significant company

restructuring, a decision had to be made regarding potential layoffs. While the financial realities were stark, my faith guided me to prioritize compassion and fairness. Instead of simply issuing

impersonal notices, I advocated for individual meetings with each affected employee, offering support, outplacement services, and personalized assistance in their job search. This wasn't about avoiding a difficult decision, but about approaching it with empathy and respect, reflecting the love and grace that I strive to live out daily. The response from the employees was remarkable. While undoubtedly saddened by the situation, they expressed deep gratitude for the dignity and respect afforded to them, a testament to the impact of a compassionate approach rooted in faith. The transition was smoother, morale improved, and the company's reputation remained relatively unscathed compared to our competitors in similar situations. Furthermore, fostering a culture of ethical behavior requires more than just reacting to situations; it necessitates proactive measures. I have instituted regular training sessions focusing on ethical decision-making, conflict resolution, and fair employment practices.

These sessions weren't simply

compliance exercises; they were opportunities to engage with employees on a deeper level, exploring the moral

implications of their work and aligning organizational goals with personal values. By integrating biblical principles of justice, compassion, and integrity into these discussions, we've created a shared understanding of ethical behavior that transcends mere rules and regulations. This proactive approach has fostered a work environment where employees feel empowered to speak up, report unethical behavior, and work together to uphold high ethical standards. This is a direct reflection of the faith-based culture I've sought to instill. It's not about imposing religious beliefs, but about fostering a climate of respect, responsibility, and integrity –values that resonate across diverse backgrounds and beliefs. Transparency is another critical aspect of embodying ethical leadership. In my experience, open and honest

communication, particularly during times of uncertainty or change, is crucial.

EMPLOYEES NEED TO UNDERSTAND the rationale behind decisions, even if they don't always agree with them. I've found that by sharing information openly and honestly, even when it's difficult, I build trust and foster a stronger sense of community. During a period of significant financial challenges, for example, I chose to be transparent about the company's financial situation with all employees. Instead of hiding behind jargon or corporate speak, I explained the challenges in plain language, outlining the steps we were

taking to address them. This transparency, while initially met with some anxiety, ultimately fostered a sense of shared responsibility and strengthened our commitment to working together through difficult times. This honesty, born from faith in God's provision, created a stronger team bond, reinforcing the trust and unity that a faith-based leadership style aims for. This is far more effective than attempting to maintain an illusion of strength and invulnerability.

ANOTHER CRUCIAL ASPECT of becoming a role model for ethical and faith-based leadership is accountability. This means admitting mistakes, owning responsibility for actions, and demonstrating a willingness to learn and grow. It's essential to cultivate a culture where mistakes are not seen as failures, but as opportunities for learning and improvement. In my experience, openly admitting a mistake or misjudgment has not diminished my authority, but rather strengthened it.

It demonstrated vulnerability, authenticity, and a commitment to continuous improvement, all traits highly valued by my team. This approach echoes the biblical principle of

confession and repentance, acknowledging our imperfections while striving towards righteousness. This openness not only fosters trust but also encourages others to take ownership of their own mistakes, creating a more responsible and accountable work environment. This is essential in fostering a healthy and positive organizational culture.

Building a positive work environment, however, goes beyond individual actions. It requires a conscious effort to cultivate a culture of respect, inclusion, and collaboration. This means creating a space where every employee feels valued, respected, and empowered to contribute their unique talents and perspectives.

My Christian faith compels me to see every employee as an individual created in God's image, deserving of dignity and respect.

This approach has manifested in initiatives like diversity and inclusion training, flexible work arrangements to accommodate individual needs and circumstances, and mentoring programs designed to support employee growth and development. These

programs are not merely check-boxes; they are integral parts of building a faith-based and ethical workplace, reflecting the value and dignity of each person within the company, as we treat each other as we believe we should be treated under God. The positive impact of this emphasis on human value is apparent in increased employee engagement, improved productivity, and a stronger sense of community. Leading with integrity also means actively challenging unethical behavior, both within and outside the organization. This might involve speaking up against discrimination, advocating for fair wages, or taking a stand against environmental harm. It requires courage, conviction, and a willingness to potentially face opposition.

However, my faith has given me the strength and conviction to do so, knowing that righteousness ultimately prevails. An example of this was when I discovered an instance of potential fraud within the company. While uncomfortable, I immediately initiated an investigation, working closely with legal and compliance to ensure a thorough and impartial review. This proactive approach, driven by a commitment to ethical conduct, prevented a potentially devastating scandal and reinforced the company's commitment to integrity. The outcome demonstrated the importance of prioritizing ethical considerations above personal gain or career advancement. In this case, the ethical decision was also the prudent one; however, faith provided the courage to act despite the potential risks. Finally, becoming a role model for ethical and faith-based leadership is an ongoing journey, not a destination. It requires constant self-reflection, a commitment to personal growth, and a willingness to seek guidance and support from mentors, colleagues, and the faith community. I regularly engage in prayer and spiritual disciplines to maintain a clear moral compass, reminding myself of the values that guide my actions and decisions. I also seek out opportunities for mentorship and coaching, not just to share my experiences, but to learn from others and continue growing in my leadership capacity. The goal is not perfection, but continuous progress, continuously striving to reflect the character of Christ in my professional life.

The impact extends far beyond my personal sphere; it shapes the culture of my team, influencing their behavior and ultimately creating a ripple effect throughout the organization and beyond. It's a journey of constant learning, growth, and seeking to reflect the principles of faith in every aspect of professional life. The rewards are profound, not only in terms of building successful teams, but also in fostering a workplace where people are treated with dignity, respect, and compassion.

Ultimately, it's about living out one's faith in a way that impacts the lives of those around them, both professionally and personally, proving that leadership with integrity and faith is not only possible, but profoundly effective. **Advocating for Christian Values in the Workplace Ethically**

Building a workplace culture that reflects Christian values while respecting the diverse beliefs of others requires a delicate balance. It's about influencing, not imposing.

My approach has always been rooted in leading by example, demonstrating the principles of faith through my actions and interactions rather than explicitly preaching. This isn't about forcing a religious agenda on colleagues; it's about embodying the spirit of

Christ in the professional sphere. One of the most powerful ways to advocate for Christian values ethically is through servant leadership. This approach prioritizes the needs of the team above personal gain, mirroring Christ's example of selfless service.

It involves actively listening to employees' concerns, empathizing with their struggles, and empowering them to reach their full potential. In practical terms, this means creating a workplace where employees feel valued, respected, and heard. It means offering support, mentorship, and opportunities for growth, fostering an environment where people can thrive, both professionally and personally. I found that leading with compassion and understanding has consistently led to improved team morale and increased productivity. For instance, when a particularly challenging project

threatened to overwhelm our team, I didn't simply delegate tasks; I actively participated alongside them, sharing the burden and offering encouragement. I organized team-building activities outside of work hours, fostering camaraderie and strengthening bonds. We had casual prayer times, but always ensured all felt welcome to partake or opt-out, demonstrating inclusivity and respect.

THESE ACTIONS WEREN'T overtly religious, but they reflected the core values of empathy, compassion, and community that are central to my faith. The result was a team that not only met the challenge but emerged stronger and more united. Another crucial aspect is fostering a culture of integrity and ethical behavior. This starts with me, setting a clear example through transparency and honesty in all dealings, whether with employees, clients, or senior management.

THIS CONSISTENT ETHICAL conduct creates a ripple effect, inspiring others to uphold similar standards. I've always emphasized fair treatment, ensuring that everyone, regardless of their background or beliefs, is treated with dignity and respect.

This involves creating clear, consistent policies, ensuring equitable opportunities for advancement, and actively addressing any instances of discrimination or harassment.

THIS COMMITMENT TO integrity isn't merely a matter of following company rules; it's a reflection of the moral compass shaped by my faith. It's about making decisions based on principles of fairness, justice, and love. In one instance, we faced a conflict between two employees, each presenting their side with strong conviction. Instead of simply siding with one party based on perceived power dynamics, I took the time to listen to both perspectives empathetically, seeking to understand the root of the disagreement. This approach, informed by a faith-based desire for reconciliation, allowed us to find a mutually acceptable solution that preserved the working relationship and fostered a sense of fairness within the team. The employees involved later remarked how valued they felt, not just in the resolution, but in the process itself. Transparency is paramount in building trust. Open communication, both within the team and with upper management, is essential for a healthy work environment. I've consistently strived for transparency in decision-making processes, explaining the rationale behind choices even when they are unpopular. This openness builds confidence and fosters a sense of shared purpose. When facing difficult decisions that may have ethical implications, I've always sought counsel, consulting with trusted colleagues, mentors, and my faith community for guidance, ensuring my decisions align with both my faith and the needs of the organization. Furthermore, conflict resolution within the workplace presents another opportunity to integrate Christian values. Approaching conflicts with patience, understanding, and a willingness to forgive mirrors the teachings of

Christ. In practice, this means actively mediating disputes, seeking to understand all perspectives, and striving for solutions that honor the dignity of all involved. While I've always applied professional conflict resolution techniques, my faith informs my approach by adding an extra layer of compassion and forgiveness, enabling me to work towards solutions that mend relationships, rather than simply resolving the immediate issue. However, advocating for Christian values in a diverse

workplace requires careful navigation. It's essential to

respect the diverse beliefs and perspectives of colleagues, avoiding any form of proselytization or coercion. While I've always been open about my faith when appropriate, I've never sought to impose my beliefs on others.

My focus has been on modeling Christian values through actions, not words. This means demonstrating love, compassion, forgiveness, and integrity in all interactions. Creating a truly inclusive environment requires intentional effort. This involves actively seeking out diverse voices, creating opportunities for employees from various backgrounds to contribute, and ensuring fair and equitable treatment for all.

I'VE FOUND THAT ACTIVELY seeking diverse opinions enriches our decision-making processes and promotes innovation.

By actively listening to the needs and perspectives of a diverse team, I've found solutions that would have been overlooked otherwise. This diverse perspective has proven invaluable in both improving our business strategies and creating a richer work environment where everyone feels valued and respected.

IN SUMMARY, ADVOCATING for Christian values in the workplace ethically involves leading by example, demonstrating servant leadership, fostering integrity and ethical behavior, promoting transparency and open communication, utilizing effective conflict resolution strategies, and nurturing a diverse and inclusive environment. It's a constant process of self-reflection, learning, and adapting, always striving to reflect the principles of Christ in every aspect of professional life.

The rewards extend beyond individual success, impacting the entire workplace culture and fostering an environment of respect, collaboration, and growth. It is a journey that requires ongoing commitment, but the impact on both individuals and organizations is undeniably profound. The goal is not to impose a religious agenda, but to build a workplace where employees feel respected, valued, and empowered to reach their full potential. This harmonious integration of faith and work creates a powerful synergy, leading to increased productivity, improved morale, and a thriving work environment. This isn't simply about faith; it's about creating a workplace where the fruits of the Spirit—love, joy, peace, patience, kindness, goodness, faithfulness, gentleness, and self-control—are palpable and contribute to a positive and productive work culture. The journey continues, and the striving for improvement is a hallmark of a faith-integrated leadership that honors both God and the people we are privileged to lead.

The Long-Term Impact of Faith Based Leadership

The ripple effect of faith-integrated leadership extends far beyond the immediate team or project. It's a legacy that shapes individuals, fosters strong teams, and ultimately influences the very fabric of an organization. When leaders consistently demonstrate integrity, empathy, and a commitment to servant leadership, they cultivate a culture of trust and mutual respect.

This, in turn, fosters a sense of belonging and shared purpose, leading to increased employee engagement and productivity. I've witnessed this firsthand, seeing teams flourish under a leadership style rooted in Christian values. The impact isn't just about bottom-line results; it's about creating an environment where people feel valued, heard, and empowered to reach their full potential, both professionally and personally. One of the most profound long-term impacts is the development of future leaders.

When leaders model faith-based principles, they unintentionally mentor and inspire those around them to adopt similar approaches. This creates a virtuous cycle, where a commitment to ethical behavior, compassion, and collaboration becomes a defining characteristic of the organization. This isn't about imposing religious beliefs, but about demonstrating the power of living out one's values in a professional context. The mentoring aspect is crucial; I've always prioritized guiding my team members, sharing both my professional and personal experiences, helping them navigate the complexities of career progression and personal growth. This mentorship wasn't just about skills development; it was about shaping character and cultivating a sense of purpose, encouraging them to discover their own leadership styles and how to integrate their personal beliefs into their work. The legacy of faith-based leadership also extends to the organization's overall reputation and brand.

A company known for its ethical practices, commitment to its employees, and dedication to social responsibility attracts and retains top talent. This, in turn, leads to a competitive advantage in the marketplace. In today's world, where consumers are increasingly conscious of a company's values and ethical standards, a strong reputation built on faith-based principles can be a powerful asset. We found that our commitment to ethical practices, transparency, and fair treatment of employees translated into a positive brand image, attracting not only prospective employees but also customers who shared our values.

This positive reputation was particularly valuable during challenging times, like economic downturns or periods of industry disruption. Our strong internal culture served as a bedrock, allowing us to weather the storms and emerge stronger. Furthermore, the long-term impact extends to the community beyond the organization's walls. When leaders demonstrate a commitment to serving others, they inspire employees to engage in acts of service and social responsibility.

This can take many forms, from volunteering in the community to supporting charitable causes. By fostering a culture of giving back, organizations can create a positive ripple effect,

contributing to the well-being of the wider community. We actively encouraged our employees to participate in

volunteer work and supported their involvement in local charities. This fostered a strong sense of community among employees and promoted a positive image of our

organization within the wider community.

The benefits

extended beyond mere goodwill; it boosted employee

morale, fostered teamwork, and enhanced the organization's reputation as a socially responsible corporate citizen. considering conflict resolution, a faith-based approach emphasizes empathy, forgiveness, and restorative justice. This isn't about avoiding conflict altogether, but about approaching disagreements with a spirit of humility and a desire to find common ground.

In the long run, this approach builds stronger relationships, fosters a more collaborative work environment, and prevents conflicts from escalating into damaging disputes. One specific instance involved a major disagreement between two key departments. Instead of resorting to punitive measures, we facilitated open communication, encouraged active listening, and guided both parties to find mutually acceptable solutions.

THE RESULT WAS NOT only the resolution of the immediate conflict but also the strengthening of the relationship between the departments, fostering greater collaboration and mutual respect in the future. The long-term benefits of faith-based leadership also include increased employee retention. When employees feel valued, respected, and supported by their leaders, they are more likely to remain with the organization for the long term.

THIS REDUCES TURNOVER costs, improves organizational stability, and allows for the development of a more experienced and knowledgeable workforce. We noticed that our employee turnover rate was significantly lower than industry averages, indicating a high level of employee satisfaction and loyalty. This translated into cost savings, increased productivity, and the accumulation of valuable institutional knowledge.

MOREOVER, A FAITH-BASED approach to leadership fosters creativity and innovation.

When people feel safe, respected, and empowered to express their ideas, they are more likely to be creative and innovative in their work. This is because a culture of trust and mutual respect removes the fear of failure and encourages experimentation. We found that our employees were more willing to take risks and propose innovative ideas, knowing that their efforts would be valued and supported, regardless of the outcome.

THIS RESULTED IN A significant increase in innovative product development and improved operational efficiency.

However, the integration of faith and leadership isn't without its challenges. One crucial aspect is maintaining a balance between personal faith and professional responsibilities. It's essential to respect the diverse beliefs of employees while upholding one's own values. This calls for thoughtful consideration, clear communication, and a commitment to inclusivity.

We addressed this by fostering a culture of mutual respect and understanding. We encouraged open dialogue on ethical considerations, emphasizing that employees from diverse backgrounds are valued and that their contributions are essential to our success. It's about integrating principles of faith into our leadership without imposing them. Another key challenge is navigating potential conflicts between religious beliefs and workplace policies. Leaders must carefully consider the ethical implications of their decisions and ensure that they

are consistent with both their faith and the legal requirements of their organization. This often involves navigating complex situations, requiring careful thought and sensitivity. In our case, this involved careful consideration of employee benefits, ensuring that our policies were inclusive and did not discriminate against any employee based on their religious beliefs. We strived to create a workplace environment where diversity was celebrated, and where individuals felt free to practice their faith without compromising their professional responsibilities. Finally, the long-term impact of faith-based leadership is a testament to the power of lived values. It's about more than just achieving business goals; it's about building a culture of integrity, empathy, and service. It's a legacy that shapes individuals, teams, and organizations for generations to come, leaving an indelible mark on the world. The ultimate success lies not just in the financial achievements of the company but in the positive impact we have on the lives of our employees and the wider community.

It's a journey of continuous learning, adaptation, and a commitment to embodying the principles of faith in every aspect of leadership. The long-term impact is a testament to the enduring power of integrity, compassion, and a deep-seated belief in the inherent worth of every individual. The rewards are immeasurable, extending beyond the workplace to impact lives and communities for years to come. This legacy of servant leadership, fostered by faith, is the most enduring and impactful aspect of leading with a Christian worldview.

Concluding Thoughts and Call to Action

The journey of integrating faith and leadership isn't a destination, but a continuous pilgrimage. It's a daily commitment to aligning our actions with our beliefs, a constant striving to reflect Christ's love and compassion in our interactions with others. As we've explored throughout this book, leading with faith isn't about imposing religious beliefs on employees; it's about embodying the principles of servant leadership, integrity, empathy, and forgiveness –values that resonate deeply with people of all backgrounds.

The impact transcends the workplace, extending to our families, our communities, and the world at large. Think back to the challenges we've discussed: navigating difficult conversations, resolving conflicts, making tough decisions, and fostering a culture of inclusivity and respect.

Each of these situations presented opportunities to demonstrate our faith in action.

REMEMBER THE IMPORTANCE of active listening, of seeking to understand others' perspectives before offering solutions. Remember the power of empathy, of placing ourselves in others' shoes and responding with compassion. Remember the transformative power of forgiveness, both for ourselves and for those who have wronged us.

These aren't merely theoretical concepts; they are the cornerstones of effective leadership, grounded in the unwavering love and grace of God.

The growth of our company from 500 to 2500 employees wasn't solely a result of strategic planning and business acumen. It was also, and perhaps primarily, a testament to the power of a unified team bound together by shared values and a sense of purpose. This unity wasn't born overnight; it was cultivated over years of consistent effort, intentional leadership, and a commitment to creating an environment where employees felt valued, respected, and empowered.

WE CELEBRATED SUCCESSES, offered support during challenges, and fostered a culture where open communication and mutual respect were the norm. This was not a coincidence. This was a conscious decision to live out our faith in the workplace. Consider the impact of a leader who consistently demonstrates humility, acknowledging their own shortcomings and seeking guidance from others. Imagine the effect of a leader who models forgiveness, extending grace even in the face of adversity.

PICTURE A LEADER WHO prioritizes the well-being of their team, both professionally and personally. These are not merely desirable qualities; they are essential components of effective leadership grounded in Christian values. They create a ripple effect that extends far beyond the individual and creates a workplace culture where individuals thrive. Beyond the practical applications, integrating faith into our leadership journey fosters a deeper sense of purpose and meaning. It provides a framework for understanding our role in the world, a compass that guides us through difficult decisions and challenges. It reminds us that our work is more than just a job; it's a calling to serve others, to make a positive impact, and to reflect God's love in all that we do. This sense of purpose provides resilience, enabling us to persevere through setbacks and maintain a positive outlook even during challenging times. The strength found in faith allows us to handle pressure and stress more effectively, allowing us to be more present and engaged leaders. But the integration of faith into leadership is not without its challenges.

THERE WILL BE TIMES when we feel overwhelmed, uncertain, or even discouraged. There will be situations where our faith is tested, where we are called to make difficult choices that require courage and conviction. It is during these moments that we must rely on prayer, seek guidance from trusted mentors and advisors, and lean on the support of our faith community. This support network is crucial in providing strength, perspective, and encouragement during challenging times.

THE JOURNEY OF INTEGRATING faith and leadership is a lifelong pursuit. It requires constant self-reflection, a willingness to learn and grow, and a commitment to embodying Christian values in every aspect of our lives. This journey is a process of continual growth, not just in our professional lives but also in our personal lives and faith. It is in everyday actions, in the seemingly small decisions, that our faith is truly reflected. It is in these moments of quiet reflection and prayer that our connection to our faith is strengthened.

Now, I challenge you, the reader, to reflect on your own leadership journey. How can you integrate your faith more fully into your approach to leadership? What specific steps can you take to embody Christian values in your interactions with employees, colleagues, and clients? Consider adopting practices such as daily prayer, Bible study, or meditation to deepen your connection with God and gain clarity and guidance in your decision-making process.

These practices are not just for personal growth; they are essential for effective leadership. Start by identifying areas where you can improve.

Are you consistently demonstrating integrity and honesty? Are you actively listening to and valuing the perspectives of your team members? Are you practicing empathy and compassion in your interactions with others? Are you fostering a culture of forgiveness and reconciliation? Honestly assess your strengths and weaknesses. Where do you excel? Where do you need growth? Be open to feedback from others.

Seek out mentors who can provide guidance and support. Remember that vulnerability is a strength.

It allows for growth and allows you to connect authentically with those around you. Furthermore, consider creating a leadership philosophy that incorporates your faith. This philosophy should serve as a guiding principle for your decisions and actions. It should inform your approach to conflict resolution, performance management, and team building. Make sure this philosophy is aligned with your values and beliefs and that it guides your actions.

Ensure it is not a stagnant document, but one that evolves and grows along with you. This will allow for flexibility and adaptation as you navigate the ever-changing landscape of the business world. Remember the stories shared throughout this book – the challenges faced, the lessons learned, and the successes achieved. These are not isolated incidents; they represent a common thread woven through the fabric of leadership. They are a testament to the transformative power of faith and the enduring impact of servant leadership.

Finally, I encourage you to share your faith-integrated leadership journey with others. Be a role model for those around you. Mentor others, guiding them on their own journeys of faith and leadership. Inspire those around you, fostering a culture of faith and leadership. By sharing your experiences and insights, you can encourage and empower others to lead with integrity, compassion, and purpose, thereby creating a ripple effect of positive change that extends far beyond the workplace.

This is not merely a professional aspiration; it is a call to action, a reflection of our faith in action, and a legacy we leave for future generations. Your faith-integrated leadership is a powerful force for good, and its impact is far-reaching and enduring. Remember that the journey of faith-integrated leadership is a lifelong process, one that demands constant reflection, growth, and a commitment to embodying Christian values in every aspect of our lives.

THIS ONGOING COMMITMENT will ultimately lead to a more fulfilling personal and professional life, enriching both our own lives and the lives of those we lead. The world needs more leaders like you, who are willing to integrate their faith into their work, leading with purpose, integrity, and unwavering compassion.

Acknowledgments

First and foremost, I offer my heartfelt thanks to God, whose unwavering grace and guidance have been the foundation of my journey—both personally and professionally. This book is a testament to His faithfulness and provision.

To my loving husband and children, your constant support, understanding, and unwavering belief in me have been

invaluable. Thank you for sacrificing so much so that I could pursue this passion. Your love and encouragement are my greatest treasures.

I am deeply grateful to my colleagues and mentors

throughout my career. Your wisdom, insights, and challenges have shaped me into the leader I am today. Your

contributions, both direct and indirect, are woven into the fabric of this book.

Glossary

This glossary defines key terms used throughout the book, providing clarity and context for both HR professionals and those new to the field.

Servant Leadership:

A leadership philosophy where the leader prioritizes the needs of their team and empowers them to achieve their full potential.

Integrity:

Adherence to moral and ethical principles; soundness of moral character.

Empathy:

The ability to understand and share the feelings of another.

Restorative Justice:

A system of criminal justice that

focuses on repairing the harm caused by crime and restoring relationships between offenders and victims.

Author Biography

Marisol Valle is a seasoned human resources professional and devoted Christian leader with more than three decades of experience guiding teams to achieve excellence. Throughout her career, she has cultivated workplace cultures rooted in growth, integrity, and inclusion. Her extensive expertise includes recruitment, employee relations, performance management, and conflict resolution. A strong advocate for ethical leadership, Marisol is committed to fostering equitable environments that honor core values and principles. Beyond her leadership roles, Marisol shares her insights as a writer and speaker, particularly on the intersection of faith and leadership. She is also the visionary behind MRSBYVALLE, a brand that seamlessly blends luxury with inspiration. Through MRSBYVALLE, Marisol empowers others on their personal and professional journeys, offering an exquisite selection of luxury home décor and more. When she's not leading teams or inspiring audiences, Marisol cherishes time with her family and actively contributes to the well-being of her community.